"A wise and witty book! Seán Brickell shows us the true meaning of confidence and how personal and professional success is so often the pursuit of a dream – in spite of experience."
Jim Stevens, blind karate champion, author & artist.

"This is a must read for anyone who wants to boost their confidence in life. Packed with practical examples, inspirational life stories and humorous anecdotes, this book is an easy and entertaining read that covers many situations where confidence, or lack of it, can really change the outcome for better or for worse."
Dominic Scarlett, HR Business Partner, Brit Insurance.

"With a great mix of humour, colourfully random anecdotes and well put advice, Seán takes on that real root cause of what holds many of us back – self-confidence. This is a great book for anyone who aspires to move outside of their comfort zone and recognises the key role increasing confidence will play in attaining their goals. *Don't Shoot – I'm Not Well!* will help you find your own path to a more confident and therefore accomplished version of yourself."
Jessica Moulton, Partner, McKinsey & Company.

"I think the book's introduction says it all for me that confidence allows someone to be their true self. Through this thoroughly absorbing book Seán Brickell makes me feel confident in just who I am. And he has, as a result, made me a better manager, friend, colleague, father, husband and leader. As the Apostle Paul said: I can do all this through him who gives me strength. I share Paul's confidence in this promise and encourage you to read this excellent book."
Chris Sutton, Head of Business Development, Royal Mail Wholesale.

"Feeling confident about yourself and what you can achieve often makes the difference between success and failure. If reading this book can help to equip you with the tools to instil confidence within yourself and those around you, then this can only assist a positive outcome!"
Daisy Berkeley, Olympic, World & European equestrian medallist.

"*Don't Shoot – I'm Not Well!* is a great read for helping you think about your confidence in situations where you really need it both in and out of work. The book is full of great stories and examples which help bring the book to life. As well as being an enjoyable read, it is useful to dip in and out of and is also a useful reference tool to help others."
Becky Ivers, Director of Organisational Development, Premier Foods plc.

"I thoroughly enjoyed reading *Don't Shoot – I'm Not Well!* It made me think, smile, laugh and question whether I'm always as confident as I could be. I'm certain this book will be of great use to many, in a personal or professional capacity, as a source of humour, inspiration or just to help them confirm that they really can achieve what they set out to do."
Barry Horgan, HR Consultant, EDF Energy.

"Sean has more self-belief and self-confidence than almost anyone I know. He writes beautifully and his whirlwind life has exposed him to a range of experiences which make this book a very good thing for people wanting to improve their self-confidence as they go about their everyday lives."
Adam Holloway, MP & ex-SAS officer.

"Even if you think you're a confident person, then you should read this book as you will learn about real and not fake confidence. And if you feel you're not a confident person then you should also read this book for the same reason. *Don't Shoot – I'm Not Well!* is not only easy to read but is really entertaining. Highly recommended."
Imran Mannan, Information Services Project Manager, Petro-Canada (UK).

"'Perhaps appropriately for someone advising about confidence Seán Brickell is brave to enter the already crowded market place of the Self Help book. Fortunately the verve and panache of his writing combined with the genuine insights he offers make his contribution to the genre stand out and demand attention."
Jon Brain, UK network TV news correspondent.

"*Don't Shoot – I'm Not Well!* is a great read that is both educational and entertaining. It is a colourful, thought-provoking, encouraging, down to earth and practical book that will make you feel you can improve your confidence. This is because it has a powerful mixture of practical tips and psychological re arch blended with moving and inspiring real life stories."
Sir Ranulph Fiennes, Explorer.

"C sedness and determination are essential to achieve success in life; but
e\ the most steely will face doubts and seemingly insurmountable
se.b cks. Sean's book looks at how to find, or re-find confidence when things
ge' ough. Getting the best rewards requires risk. Séan's book will inspire
m people to take the plunge with greater confidence."
Si ames Dyson, Inventor.

"C fidence is the foundation of every successful endeavour. Here's your
bl rint."
D: Magliano, ex-Marketing Director for London 2012 & ex-Director
of mercial and Marketing at England 2018.

"N ter who we are, self-doubt, lack of self-belief and the temptation to
he e council of our fears afflict all of us at times. Whether in everyday
sit s, or the bigger events in our lives, Seán Brickell tackles the issue of
se nfidence head-on in this highly readable book. *Don't Shoot – I'm Not*
W es practical examples and inspirational case studies to provide an
ex ely apposite confidence handrail which is so often essential to finding
th ner-self assurance necessary to overcome the obstacles of life's assault
co
Lt ol Stuart Tootal DSO OBE, ex-Commanding Officer of 3rd Battalion of
the arachute Regiment in Afghanistan.

"Confidence is often the differentiator between success and failure in life. And that is still very much the case for women in today's society, both personally and professionally. Seán Brickell provides a refreshing and often hilarious perspective on the issue and opportunity, both from a male as well a more surprising female point of view."
Jennifer Philpot, Global Director of Recruitment and Employer Brand,
Ernst & You

XB00 000009 5767

"Great title. Great book. And a great read on an important subject that affects all of us. *Don't Shoot - I'm Not Well!* is a thought-provoking, tell it as it is read that will amuse, move and motivate you to make a difference in your life."
Doug Richard, Entrepreneur & ex-Dragon on BBC TV's *Dragons' Den*.

"As an HR professional in the finance industry I know how important both personal and professional confidence is, whatever your role or position. *Don't Shoot – I'm Not Well!* is an excellent and entertaining guide about how to acquire it and the real life stories throughout the book also make this book a must read."
Mandy Said, HR Director HSH Nordbank.

"In today's complex, challenging and hyper-competitive world it can be tough trying to achieve success. One of the most important elements on the road to achieving success is the belief in yourself. For those seeking to develop their inner potential, Seán's book is a must read. *Don't Shoot - I'm Not Well!* is jam-packed with fascinating insights into how to develop self-confidence. It is a timely, compelling and a no-nonsense guide which is easy to follow, all based on real experiences. It has clearly been written by someone who knows what they're talking about. The advice and techniques contained within the book are prescient and insightful. Indeed, they reflect those that I have found myself using in many high risk situations. So I know they work!"
Nick Cameron MC MBE, ex-Sergeant in 22 SAS.

"This is a book that will give women confidence as much as it will men, whether emotionally, socially or professionally. Séan Brickell not only knows what he's talking about, but also really cares about helping you gain greater confidence so you believe in yourself more, with all the good things that will achieve for you."
Pauline Vickers, Head of Sales Support, Bids and Solutions, Royal Mail.

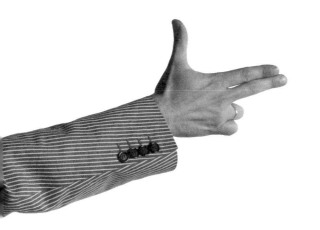

DON'T
SHOOT
I'M NOT
WELL!

Visit our How To website at **www.howto.co.uk**

At **www.howto.co.uk** you can engage in conversation with our authors - all of whom have 'been there and done that' in their specialist fields. You can get access to special offers and additional content but most importantly you will be able to engage with, and become a part of, a wide and growing community of people just like yourself.

At **www.howto.co.uk** you'll be able to talk and share tips with people who have similar interests and are facing similar challenges in their lives. People who, just like you, have the desire to change their lives for the better - be it through moving to a new country, starting a new business, growing their own vegetables, or writing a novel.

At **www.howto.co.uk** you'll find the support and encouragement you need to help make your aspirations a reality.

How To Books strives to present authentic, inspiring, practical information in their books. Now, when you buy a title from How To Books, you get even more than just words on a page.

DON'T SHOOT I'M NOT WELL!

Confidence for when you _really_ need it

 BRICKELL

howtobooks

Published by How To Books Ltd,
Spring Hill House, Spring Hill Road
Begbroke, Oxford OX5 1RX. United Kingdom.
Tel: (01865) 375794 Fax: (01865) 379162
info@howtobooks.co.uk
www.howtobooks.co.uk

How To Books greatly reduce the carbon footprint of their books by
sourcing their typesetting and printing in the UK.

British Library Cataloguing in Publication Data.
A catalogue record for this book is available from the British Library.

ISBN: 978 1 84528 457 2

Cover design by Baseline Arts Ltd
Cartoons by David Mostyn
Produced for How To Books by Deer Park Productions, Tavistock
Typeset by Baseline Arts Ltd
Printed and bound in Great Britain by Bell and Bain Ltd, Glasgow

NOTE: The material contained in this book is set out in good faith for
general guidance and no liability can be accepted for loss or expense
incurred as a result of relying in particular circumstances on statements
made in the book. Laws and regulations are complex and liable to change,
and readers should check the current position with the relevant authorities
before making personal arrangements.

Contents

People to thank...

I want to thank the people who have helped me lick this book into a readable shape. My literary lieutenants, who gave me their honest and useful feedback, include Sally, my wife and random thinker in residence, the irrepressible and orange-wearing Corjanne van Drimmelen, the equally irrepressible and impassioned Dr Irene Lopez de Vallejo, the calmly cerebral Dominic Scarlett, the honest and delightful Donna Tingley, the practical and big-haired Paul Collins, the feisty and straight-talking Eleanor Price and, very importantly, Joanna Brickell (aka Mum) for her ever sharp eye for superlative syntax!

Then, thanks of course go to my publisher Giles Lewis, his Editorial Director Nikki Read and their Publicity Manager Katie Read for their sterling work as well as my Copy Editor Rebecca Wilson and Production Manager Bill Antrobus.

I would of course also like to thank all those who contributed to the book as well as the people who, in several cases, made that happen and endured my polite persistence in getting to chat with the people I needed to.

And I would also like to thank all makers of truly gorgeous chocolate cakes and biscuits for providing the fabulous fuel to help me in my moments of literary and creative need!

Introduction

Your levels of confidence can make your life either wondrously worthwhile or witheringly worthless. It is that crucial. But confidence is not, as so many people believe, about being a wise-cracking, somersaulting, swashbuckling, Oscar award-winning extrovert. In fact, some of the quietest people you come across are among the most confident.

It's actually about having true confidence. In short, it's about being reconciled to who you really are, being at peace with yourself and being understanding of and comfortable with all the beautiful, beastly and even bizarre aspects of your character and how you deal with the different challenges life throws at you.

This is an essential life skill and state of mind about which I've become fascinated since I was a child because of my own experiences and the experiences of others. I know what it is like to have little to no confidence and believe that you're not going to be able to tackle and overcome a challenge and even enjoy that challenge. I have felt the deceptively subtle, yet overwhelmingly strong fear of failure. I know the cruel and unreliable comfort that comes from finding seemingly reassuring reasons for why you were not destined to do or achieve something which can invariably prompt you not to try. And all this and other aspects of a lack of confidence stop us so easily from living the life we want to … a life we have too little time to make the most of.

So why am I writing this book? Indeed, who am I to be writing this book? I've come across too many people over the years who've denied themselves so much in the short term and long term because of a lack of confidence, whether temporary or ingrained. And my own experiences have taught me a lot too. Overcoming a lack of confidence and gaining it when I've been determined to overcome any challenges and fears so I can succeed, or at least have a damn good go at succeeding, have played a significant part in my life. It has also played a central role in the lives of the varied people, both well known and unknown, to whom I've spoken for this book.

I overcame a crippling childhood fear of speaking in public and I am now asked to speak professionally to diverse audiences around the world, sometimes in front of thousands of people. I taught myself how to throw the discus from reading books and went on to win various UK county championships and junior international honours even though, and certainly at international competition level, a lot of the other boys were bigger than me and had been properly trained by a coach.

I got my first journalism job, reporting for my local newspaper aged 14. I later became the youngest ever network TV news reporter in the UK, aged 21, and a year later became a network TV newsreader. I have interviewed heads of state and movie stars and have also been stuck right in the middle of violent riots as a journalist. I've completed some unnerving assignments as an undercover investigative journalist, sometimes at great risk of general unpleasantness if I'd been uncovered. I once managed to talk my way out of being held at gunpoint while travelling through a war-torn country and even managed to bluff my way through 13 security checks to gain access to the former Soviet Union leader Mikhail Gorbachev.

I set up the first of my two businesses with no financial backing and no knowledge of how to start, let alone run a business. Yet within three to four years I was earning a six-figure income and travelling the globe to work with and meet a diverse range of people in some of the world's most high profile companies. And all this was due to developing my confidence so I could achieve, or at least have a go at achieving, what I wanted to in life.

For the first few years of my entrepreneurial life I had setbacks and failures and what I call 'head in my hands' moments when I thought that the money was about to run out and the business was about to die an undignified death. But I always knew I was doing the right thing. I believed that I would pull it off and I certainly needed all my confidence to persevere and then prevail.

When I was successful, my confidence grew, not just because I had achieved a professional, financial or personal accolade, but because I had succeeded when others, including myself sometimes, hadn't always thought I would make it. And it's that contrasting feeling of having overcome the seemingly overwhelming challenges and then succeeded that is the most satisfying because it proves to you what you can achieve and how much you will grow as a person – a more confident and capable person.

I have spent many years meeting and talking with people, both personally and professionally, who, no matter how confident they might appear to be or how important their professional or social position might suggest they are, lack the necessary confidence to be what they want to be or to achieve what they need to. Those experiences have inspired this book to help you and others enjoy finding out about what confidence really is – and isn't – and also how to believe in yourself in a variety of different real life scenarios. Most importantly, this book will help you to go out and have a crack at what you want to with greater levels of confidence.

The various scenarios covered include how to be confident when starting up your own business, dealing with difficult or lecherous colleagues, being made redundant, dealing with alpha males, dating work colleagues, women asking men out, feeling good when naked, sexual confidence, coping with various setbacks and making significant life changes. The final chapter provides guidance on sustaining confidence in the long term, to build on what this book will also give you in the short term.

You can pick and choose what subjects you will enjoy learning from at the time you need to do so. As well as being packed with lots of jargon-free advice that really works and will work for you, I've also wanted to make this book light-hearted as I believe learning is greatly enhanced if you can smile and laugh about life.

Why complicate something and try to make it drainingly lofty when you can make it more understandable and engaging? The latter is much more likely to enable and inspire you to believe in yourself and do something about what you need and want to achieve. The worthiness of the message is there but it's more understandable and therefore easier to apply.

This book is highly practical and is free of often baffling psychological language. Knowing about your sub-modalities and predicates and whether or not you should adhere to the Milton model isn't really going to help you achieve better confidence. It is laid out simply and structured so that you can dip into and out of different sections, depending on what your needs are. There are many practical points and exercises you can use that will make a difference; but only if you act upon them and then go out and put your newly found confidence skills into practice.

Also included are lots of real life stories from the well known and unknown about what part confidence has played in their lives, their setbacks and successes, and how they've learned to develop confidence, as a result, and then go on to achieve what was right for them. They are all thought provoking and inspiring. And they are, like the contents of this book, honest, real, enlightening, energising and empowering.

It's also important to refer to self-esteem, as opposed to self-confidence. Although they sound similar in concept, there is one key difference between them. Self-confidence is how capable you appear to feel, whereas self-esteem is about how capable you feel you really are when you don't have to put on an appearance for others. Although it's easier to be or appear to be self-confident than have high self-esteem, the thoughts you think, the feelings you have and the actions you take will determine your levels of self-confidence and self-esteem.

For the purpose of this book, I will be referring to confidence rather than self-esteem, for simplicity and also to save any possible confusion. This is because the empowering techniques and stories will have a beneficial effect on both your self-confidence and self-esteem as they are both interlinked.

My belief and hope is that, by reading this book, you will not only feel and want to feel more genuinely confident, but will then put everything you read into practice so that both your self-esteem and self-confidence will start improving immediately.

Part One

The reality of our confidence

Introduction

- 91% OF US ARE NOT LIVING LIFE TO ITS FULL POTENTIAL.

- 77% OF US BELIEVE THAT CONFIDENCE IS THE MAIN CONTRIBUTORY FACTOR IN ACHIEVING SUCCESS.

- 72% OF US BELIEVE THAT ACQUIRING CONFIDENCE IS POSSIBLE.

- 46% OF US BELIEVE THAT CONFIDENCE WILL COMPLETELY TRANSFORM OUR LIVES.

- 62% BELIEVE MEN ARE MORE CONFIDENT THAN WOMEN PROFESSIONALLY.

Confidence gives you the impetus and therefore the self-belief to grasp opportunities in life so you can enjoy them and even succeed when you might not have otherwise. Therefore you can find new and deeper ways of fulfilling your potential to achieve happiness, success and stronger self-esteem.

In a survey I conducted of men and women aged 18–70, a massive 91% believed that we're not living life to its full potential. The survey shows that we're allowing too many of life's opportunities and pleasures to slip us by even though we have so many things we want to enjoy and achieve: potential love, potential personal happiness, potential professional success, potential financial wealth, potential adventure and, of course, so much of the colour and variety of life itself.

And, with more confidence, the men and women questioned said they would want greater inner peace more than they would want more money, a nicer partner or a better job. More than 40% of people felt that having the right confidence would completely transform their lives.

That's why 40% of respondents said that they feel inspired by truly confident people. And about three-quarters of those surveyed felt that acquiring confidence is possible.

In fact, I'll put it even more bluntly. The lives most of us are missing out on are the goals, hopes and desires that we REALLY want and need to make our existence more complete and worthwhile. And those are the ones that require confidence so we can enable ourselves to have a go at achieving something which we can later look back on with contentment and, as a result, a greater sense of confidence.

The reassuring reality is that confidence is not a constant; it's a variable. This means that it's very hard to be completely confident in all situations all of the time. But effort is required, as is courage and a vision of the sort of life you want. Having the right amount of confidence will enable you to triumph in what you want to, and not having enough of it can leave your hopes and dreams trounced. In your life it is the difference between creating substance and enduring scarcity.

Chapter 1

The core of confidence

- SELF-CONFIDENCE IS PRIMARILY A STATE OF MIND.

- SELF-CONFIDENCE IS ALWAYS RELATIVE TO THE TASK AND SITUATION.

- SELF-CONFIDENCE IS NEITHER ABSOLUTE NOR FINAL.

- SELF-CONFIDENCE IS ACHIEVABLE.

- SELF-CONFIDENCE IS LIFE CHANGING.

- SELF-ESTEEM IS HOW YOU REALLY FEEL ABOUT YOURSELF ON THE INSIDE.

First things first. Self-esteem and self-confidence are related, but different. Self-confidence is what gives you the impetus to behave in a certain way or go for something you want. It's about how you appear to feel about yourself to the outside world. Self-esteem is about how you truly feel about yourself, on the inside, when no one's looking.

A study in America found that 96% of 4 year olds had high self-esteem and a strong self-image. These children believed there were no limits to what they could do or enjoy. But revealingly the study showed that by the time they reached 18, less than 5% had a good self-image. Although dispiriting, it's hardly surprising because of the emotional, physical, cultural and general and unpredictable assault course that life takes us on from a young age.

That's why your state of mind will determine much of what happens to you emotionally, mentally, physically, professionally, financially, socially and in all aspects of your life. In essence, what you perceive about yourself is what you transmit to other people. So if you feel that you're a leaden and lumpy lummock, with all the appeal of one, then that's the impression you'll give to other people even if you then try to pretend that you're not.

People will instinctively and subconsciously pick up all this and, despite your best efforts to the contrary, you will make their unconscious mind, and therefore them, feel that you are indeed … a leaden and lumpy lummock. And, when they don't want to hang out with you or even try to give you a piggyback, for instance, then you'll know why. This in turn will make you feel less confident about yourself, which will then confirm your initially negative self-image and the image of you they hold in their minds. And so it goes on.

Now, confidence is always relative to the task and situation. That's why we have different levels of confidence in different scenarios. For example, you might feel confident meeting someone on a one-to-one basis but feel very unconfident in a crowd of people, and yet you want to make more friends. This lack of confidence in groups will affect your being able to meet more people. Having said that, there are some people who can quite easily mix with a group, but don't always feel comfortable on a one-to-one basis. Such people are not at ease because, in a one-to-one scenario, they're putting themselves in a position where there is a greater focus on them and what they feel, think and say than when they're in a group where any focus is more diffuse. Of course, unless they really don't like the person they're with on a one-to-one basis, then feeling ill at ease with the more gently intense one-to-one scenario is a sign that their self-esteem and confidence may well be lacking.

Self-confidence is situational and relative and is not absolute and final. It depends on the situation, on you and your attitude at the time. Just because Roger Federer is one of the greatest tennis players of all time, because he has won more majors than anyone else, doesn't mean he's always going to feel on top emotional and mental and therefore physical form. There have been numerous times when he's been beaten – even by a British player! – because his confidence levels fluctuated unhelpfully.

But although self-confidence is primarily situational, it can be applied by a person generally across an area of their life if they have strong confidence in one aspect of that field.

For example, if you're good at rugby then you are more likely to have a higher level of confidence in other ball and running sports, even though they may have different rules, aims and differently shaped balls. This is because you have proved yourself in your chosen sport and therefore you're more likely to believe that you can compete and succeed to a good level in other sports. Generally, it is a good predictor of how well people will perform on all sorts of tasks. High self-confidence also increases people's motivation and persistence.

Self-confidence and self-esteem are achievable, but you have to believe that they are before you can even contemplate improving your own. If you don't believe confidence is achievable then your conscious mind will programme your unconscious mind accordingly. And so even if you read and use this book or go on one of my masterclasses, to put into practice what you have learned, then you'll make it much harder for yourself. Remember that confidence is situational and relative and not final or absolute. You cannot be confident at absolutely everything all of the time. But you can and will be confident at some of the things in your life that are important to you, whether it's the way you conduct yourself in your marriage or the way you feel about your competence to do your job to a very high standard.

Foundations of confidence

The foundations of confidence are:

- COURAGE

- ACTION

- DETERMINATION

- RESILIENCE

- BELIEF

- ACCEPTANCE

- PERSISTENCE

- GOAL PLAN

Courage

Courage is the fuel for action. It is the thing that gives your deed the impetus it needs both to start and to sustain the action no matter how much that challenge frightens you or beats you back. And after the deed has been done, whether you have succeeded or failed, your courage is the ingredient that will have strengthened your resolve and your right to feel proud in having pursued something that others have been too timid to try. And that in itself sets you above those people and should rightly increase your confidence.

The US diplomat Eleanor Roosevelt once remarked: 'You gain strength, courage and confidence by every experience in which you really stop to look fear in the face. You are able to say to yourself, "I have lived through this horror. I can take the next thing that comes along." You must do the thing you think you cannot do.'

REAL LIFE STORY

Through my professional and personal life I have met quite a few truly inspiring people, many of whom displayed courage in adversity. These were ordinary people who, in some cases, did extraordinary things. One such person was Caroline Tucker, then a 12-year-old schoolgirl. I came across her on one of my first stories as a young national newspaper reporter.

A fire had engulfed the council house she lived in with her family on a poor housing estate in Swansea in Wales. The parents had managed to get out with all but one of their children, their 4-year-old daughter Amanda. Caroline realised this and rushed back into the house to rescue her little sister. By then, her home was well ablaze and Caroline braved temperatures of 700 degrees Celsius. She was unable to save Amanda, but in the process received the most horrific burns to more than 75% of her body. She was lucky not to have perished as well.

Caroline survived but was shockingly disfigured. After the six months she spent in hospital undergoing constant surgery and treatment, I went back to see the family to talk to Caroline to see how she was and how her life had been. When she came into their living room on that sunny weekday morning it was all I could do not to show any sign of the stomach-churning horror I felt seeing the repulsive injuries she bravely endured.

Her mouth, ears, nose and eyelids had all melted. The doctors had drilled two small holes where her nose had been, had cut a slit where her mouth had been and created two further holes where her ears had been. Her hands had been so disfigured by the heat that they were bent back and were barely usable. The skin all over her body was a painful patchwork of red, raw flesh that had been burnt and had peeled away and blistered horribly.

But despite being in a lot of pain and needing constant and excruciating treatment she was trying to smile and be positive. She had a dignity and a composure that was as humbling as it was profoundly moving and inspiring. I remember her mother later telling me that when her closest friends first saw her, as I was seeing her, they all ran away screaming and crying and hadn't been back since.

Yet Caroline had a gentle matter-of-fact confidence about what she had done at the time of the fire when she ran into that blazing house, facing death or disfigurement and, despite the shocking consequences of her outstanding courage, she was also still confident about her future and how her life wasn't going to be impaired by her injuries. Not surprisingly Caroline won various accolades including receiving a national UK Child of Courage award from the then Princess of Wales who cried when she met Caroline as she was so profoundly moved by this extraordinary young girl.

So if, for instance, you're fretting about asking someone out or resigning from a job you hate because you're afraid you might not find another or you have to compete against someone who appears better than you, remember Caroline's courage, not just at the time of the fire, but also afterwards. A lot of people would have given up if they had been Caroline and operated with little to no confidence for the rest of their lives. But she has not taken that path. She has shown that ordinary people can do extraordinary things and that, if we really want to achieve something, we all have the potential courage to do so. It's just a matter of how much we want to succeed and whether we decide to tap into our potential for courage.

Action

Taking action is an essential ingredient for both acquiring and sustaining confidence, let alone for life itself. There's no point in thinking and even saying how you're going to go for that or achieve this or enjoy the other if you don't do anything about it. Even if you feel you don't have the confidence to actually take action, then try to see beyond the deed itself. Taking just one small step or action to achieve one small result will help you achieve much more than one small boost to your confidence, certainly over time.

Take this simple example: You want a pay rise because you think you're worth it and need one to help improve your life. You earn £35,000 pa. If, despite feeling nervous, you sum up enough confidence to ask for a 10% pay rise, for example, and you actually get it, you've just got yourself an extra £3,500 pa. That's £3,500 you would not now be able to enjoy if you had not taken action. And it's worth adding that that 10% boost will not just be a financial one. It will add at least 10% to your confidence and your determination to be more confident again and to believe in yourself.

We like things that are familiar and that bring us comfort, but this way our brains are less likely to take notice of what we're doing. And that can lead to inaction out of being nestled snugly in our comfort zones. The more comfortable we get the longer we can become used to not testing our confidence levels and that decreases our motivation.

It's like a talented athlete who's excellent at their sport at their level, but who never progresses to a higher and more rewarding level for fear that it might be too challenging for them and that they might fail. Their inaction just makes life that much easier for the people they've been competing against who do strive for something that can grow their confidence as much as it will challenge them.

But when, after a protracted period of not taking action, we need to leave that comfort zone to achieve something, we meet a greater challenge than if we took action more regularly. On the other hand, when we experience something new and testing, certainly if it's rewarding and pleasurable, then our brains will release dopamine, a chemical which motivates us to seek reward. This will further your mental desire to take action and therefore put yourself in the arena of life rather than sit out of sight on the sidelines as a passive spectator.

If, before taking action, you could travel into the future to experience the results of what you were initially afraid to do then you would feel how much more confident you will become because you took even one small step – a deed that is far outweighed by the net result of actually doing something.

Taking action and having the confidence to do so can take many forms. But it can and invariably will achieve results, as the following charmingly light-hearted and simple tale shows.

As Casanova lay on his deathbed, there was a commotion at his bedroom door. A young man was insisting that he speak to the famous man because he had a question only Casanova could answer. Even though Casanova's doctor pointed out that only family and close friends could see him, the great man asked that the visitor be let in.

The young man knelt at his bedside and said: 'Casanova, you have made love to more than 1,200 of the most beautiful women in Italy.'

Casanova looked at him and said: '1,500, actually.'

'Alright,' said the young man, 'You have made love to more than 1,500 of the most beautiful women in Italy. But how did you do it?'

Casanova asked him to come closer and whispered in his ear: 'I asked!'

Casanova took action and got … well, a lot more … ahem … action. He just did it and had a go. And this is one of the most important pillars of confidence because you can plan, discuss, believe in yourself, accept your strengths and your weaknesses and be determined, but they mean very little if you don't just go out and try to do what you want to achieve.

REAL LIFE STORY

Eric 'Rizen' Lynch is an American professional poker player and is someone who typifies taking action, even if it means risking failure. His poker career really started when he won the Million Dollar Guaranteed Tournament at PokerStars in 2006. His winning trend continued when he made it to 52+ final tables on PokerStars alone. His online winnings amount to more than US$1.3 million.

'In my professional life, confidence is everything. In poker, the difference between a winning player and a losing player is not all that big, and it's a game where you are constantly being both negatively impacted by good plays (bad beats, unlucky draws, etc.) and being positively impacted by bad plays (when you make a bad play but get lucky and deliver the bad beat),' said Eric.

'Being able to separate the results from the actions and truthfully look back and know if you're making good plays or bad plays takes a huge amount of confidence in your game and knowing what is right and wrong. Conversely, executing the correct plays at the table takes a ton of confidence in your ability to read the other players, put them on accurate hand ranges, and then make the correct play, even when at times it can be risky.

'In my personal life, confidence has been huge as well. To be really blunt, my wife is completely out of my league, but I had the confidence in myself and what I had to offer as a person to ask her out anyway. I left a six figure a year job as a software engineer after six years to become a professional poker player purely based on the confidence I had in myself to succeed if I put my mind to it.

'That was in 2006 and, over $3.5 million in cash wins later, it's a decision I'll never regret. But the idea of leaving a steady, good paying job to tackle a career filled with risk took a great degree of confidence in myself and my abilities. It helped that I also had a lot of confidence that, should it not work out, I could always get another software engineering job again!'

And Eric added: 'What would I say to someone whose lack of confidence is adversely affecting their life? I would tell them to take a chance. I think the biggest reason that people are not confident is they fear failure. Because they fear failure they'd rather settle for mediocrity and never have to worry about failing or rejection, but they also never give themselves the chance to experience greatness.

'I would rather be confident in myself and go out on a limb and deal with failure and give myself a chance to experience greatness than settle for mediocrity and never truly find out what I'm capable of simply because I lacked the confidence to take a chance.'

Determination

If you really want something in your life, like confidence or happiness or more money or a great life partner, then you need to really want to go out and try to make it happen and, most importantly, keep on trying to make it happen, even when things don't go to plan.

Action is one thing, but you not only need the determination to take action in the first place but to keep taking it, certainly when you're faced with a setback. And the latter is much harder to sustain, certainly when your confidence is tested. But determination will see you through because even if you don't achieve exactly what you set out to do – the chances are, though, that you will – then you will gain greater confidence from the fact that you kept at it. And that will give you strength.

I know about this to the extent that I nearly died doing something that was unlike almost any other challenge I had faced physically and mentally.

I had just collapsed out of sheer physical exhaustion on the icily cold and snow-hardened face of South East Asia's highest mountain. I had been ill and had not slept properly for four days and nights on a mountaineering expedition that was testing my physical and mental toughness, resolve, belief and courage. And yet I wasn't a mountaineer. I was someone who, at just four weeks' notice, was offered a testing and life-changing challenge that was way beyond my technical, physical and mental comfort zone.

As I lay on my back, physically weak and mentally exhausted, there was this growing part of me that knew there was no comfortable way out of my wretched position whichever way I went. We were on the south face of the remote 16,502 ft Carstensz Pyramid in West Papua (formerly Irian Jaya) in Indonesia. My three friends and I were experiencing the worst weather in the region for nearly half a century. I had already started getting a mild form of frostbite in my toes. Then one of the guys above me shouted down: 'It doesn't get any easier Seán. In fact, it gets a lot tougher. You're not going to make it. We can pick you up on the way down.'

That made me sink even further into a miserable morass. But then I thought of those who mean the most to me – my family and my true friends. I wanted them to feel proud of me. I didn't want to let them down by being the only one who didn't make it to the summit which, at that time, only about 200 people had ever reached.

The climb was way beyond my level of technical climbing ability. Previously, I didn't even know what the climbing difficulty rating (HVS 5.9) meant. HVS stands for Hard Very Severe – or, as I was to term it later: High Very Stupid! I and another team member asked an SAS climbing instructor to give us a crash course beforehand. When he found out what little experience we had, which mountain we were tackling and the limited time left before we attempted to conquer it, he replied: 'There's no point in trying to teach you anything at this stage as you're either mad or suicidal – if not both.'

Back on the mountainside I sat there for 10 minutes churning over what to do. I reflected on what, in every respect, had been a very hard journey to get to my end goal and how I would hate myself if I took the easy option and quit before I achieved my aim because of the soul-sapping setbacks. I then forced myself to imagine the elation of reaching the summit, making all that I had endured along the way seem worth it. It was then that I took a gamble and drank most of my water supply to give me that last gasp of strength to have one final crack at a prize that appeared to me, and certainly others, to be out of my reach.

For the next two hours I stormed up the sometimes sheer mountain face, ignoring the physical and mental torments, with a renewed sense of determination and actually caught up with the others who were stunned. Their delight at seeing what I had somehow achieved spurred me on even further. We reached the summit about an hour later.

I just couldn't stop grinning. I had achieved something that, before the expedition, I didn't know I was capable of accomplishing and, once the challenge was underway, I doubted I was ever going to succeed at. I took a risk by tackling the trip. Shortly after collapsing I narrowly escaped death during a massive rockfall while clinging to a sheer rock face. But this challenge was a gamble that opened me up to new possibilities that have strengthened my belief in myself to succeed. And that has led to new achievements which were realised with a stronger sense of determination because I know what I can attain if I stick with it.

Resilience

The human mind, spirit and body can withstand a lot of psychological and physical punishment. Confident people tend to be mentally resilient. They accept that life varies and that they will experience good and bad, but they are determined to withstand the tough times so they can recognise, enjoy and thrive during better periods. And this will give you a head start because, by being resilient, you are strengthening your mind and heart to the extent that you will get better at dealing with setbacks.

Studies have confirmed the association between resilience and positive emotion.[1] Examining the role positive emotion plays in resilience, one piece of research found that widows with high levels of resilience experience more positive (e.g. peaceful) emotions than those with low levels of resilience. It also found that the resilient widows were more able to control their positive emotional experiences to recover and bounce back from daily stress. In this case, some studies argue[2] that positive emotions help resilient people to build psychological resources for themselves that are necessary for coping successfully with a significant catastrophe, such as the 9/11 terrorist attacks in the USA.

By examining people's emotional responses to the events of 9/11, research suggests that positive emotions are critical to developing resilience and act to buffer people from depression after such crises. Moreover, highly resilient people were more likely to notice positive meanings within the problems they faced (e.g. they felt grateful to be alive), endured fewer depressive symptoms and experienced more positive emotions after the terrorist attacks than people of low resilience.

Moreover, those with low resilience exhibit difficulties with regulating negative emotions and are susceptible to adverse reactions when they experience daily stresses.[3] They are likely to believe that there is no end for the unpleasant experience of daily stresses and they may have higher levels of stress. In general, resilient people are believed to possess positive emotions, and such emotions in turn influence their responses to adversity.

REAL LIFE STORIES

Here are some examples of famous success stories that show how important resilience is and how much you can achieve through it.

■ The Hollywood film director George Lucas spent four years shipping the script for *Star Wars* around the various studios and racking up numerous rejections in the process. If he'd let his negative inner voice get to him he would never have ended up with one of the highest grossing films of all time.

■ Albert Einstein was considered an 'unteachable' fool by his early teachers.

■ The professional basketball legend Michael Jordan was cut from his high school basketball team. He later said: 'I've failed over and over again in my life, and that is why I succeed.'

■ Ludwig van Beethoven's music teacher told him he was a hopeless composer.

■ Colonel Sanders (creator of Kentucky Fried Chicken) was told 'no' by more than 1,000 restaurants for more than a year while he lived in his car trying to sell his chicken recipe.

■ Thomas Edison is known as one of the most prolific inventors in history holding 1,093 US patents as well as many patents in the UK, France and Germany. When the inventor of the light bulb and the movie camera was four he was sent home from school with a note. The note told his mother that she was to remove her son from school because he was 'too stupid to learn'. Edison's mother decided to teach him herself. He only had three months of formal schooling yet went on to create numerous inventions such as the phonograph. He was also partially deaf in one ear.

■ Walt Disney was turned down by over 100 banks when he tried to get funding to develop Disneyland. He was also fired from his job at a newspaper for 'lacking ideas'. He also had several bankruptcies before he was able to develop Disneyland.

■ Fred Astaire, regarded as one of the greatest dancers and film musical performers in history, kept a memo over his fireplace from an MGM testing director after his first screen test that said: 'Can't act. Can't sing. Slightly bald. Can dance a little.'

■ Enrico Caruso, the famous opera singer, was told by his teacher that he had no voice at all and couldn't sing.

■ Mark Victor Hansen and Jack Canfield, the authors of the *Chicken Soup for the Soul* series, were turned down by 50 book publishers before somebody finally agreed to take a chance. They have since sold more than 75 million copies.

REAL LIFE STORY

Colonel Stuart Tootal won the Distinguished Service Order (DSO) for his bravery in battle, as well as being awarded an OBE in recognition of his military leadership. It was the culmination of a distinguished 20-year career in the military.

He commanded the 3rd Battalion of the British Parachute Regiment in some of the fiercest fighting in the war in Afghanistan. 3 PARA was the first UK unit to be sent into Helmand province where the aspiration to conduct a peace mission was replaced by participating in a level of combat that has not been experienced by the British Army since the Korean War. He and his men had to adapt and overcome, despite a flawed mission, significant casualties and an almost complete lack of resources.

Being elite troops, they were at the forefront of the protracted battle and lived and fought in tough and dangerous conditions, often wearing the same clothes for months on end, while constantly under attack from the Taliban. Improvised Explosive Devices (IEDs) and mines were just some of the most significant threats to the lives and morale of these men, because of their savage unpredictability and their psychological impact which had to be faced every time they went out on patrol. They never knew if an IED might be detonated as they passed it, either killing or maiming them horribly, as many such devices had already done to their comrades. Overcoming the threat required training, courage, self-confidence and strong leadership at all levels.

'Self-confidence is a fundamental of all you do in life. Sometimes it is there without thinking about it and occasionally it is not. At times we can all feel riven by a degree of self-doubt and you need to be able to recognise this, overcome it and crack on. Once a decision has been made and one is in physical or mental forward motion self-confidence usually returns quickly,' said Stuart.

'In places like Afghanistan where you are responsible for the lives of others and everyone is looking to you to lead, you have to overcome any self-doubt by remembering who you are. The fact that your people rely on you to deliver for them helps. Thus, you put any doubts about your own confidence to the back of your mind and focus on what you get paid to do. It helps generate confidence in yourself and others draw from it. That gives you a boost and helps you to overcome your fears and get on with what you need to do.

'Military training helps generate self-confidence. A classic example is parachute training and the fear it generates when making a jump. Faith in your training and the knowledge you draw from it helps dispel fear and a lack of confidence in what you are about to do and contributes to making sure that you get through the door of an aircraft without hesitation.

'It is an approach to discipline and training that can be applied to other more general challenges in life, especially if you remember previous experiences and things that you have faced where you have felt self-doubt and lacked confidence. You regain confidence by remembering that, when you have faced similar challenges in the past, you overcame them, endured and succeeded. In essence, you say to yourself "I have been here before and I will be okay."'

Belief

Believe that you can acquire more confidence and you will. But you have to programme your mind to make this a reality and stick at it. This is for the simple reason that the more you believe in something, the more likely it is to happen. You are in effect clearing a path that you may have previously thought was too blocked with psychological obstacles or even didn't exist at all. And once you start you have to continue believing that you will acquire more confidence. This is tested most acutely when something happens that knocks your confidence. Even something minor can veer you off course and make you doubt your chosen path to confidence. That is when you need to believe.

From the age of 14, I started writing articles for my local newspaper in my school holidays as I had decided that I was going to be a network TV news reporter and newsreader and a national newspaper reporter. When I was 19 I won a place at one of the UK's top journalism colleges, beating about 3,000 people for one of 34 places on the one-year course. It was a crucial launch pad for my professional ambitions because I knew that journalism and broadcasting were my vocation.

I was more single-minded than anyone else I knew. It was as if I had had an epiphany and was messianic in my pursuit of my life's dream. But then, a month or so into this one-year course, my journalism lecturer took me aside – it was a grey Monday afternoon – and said to me (I remember it as if it were yesterday): 'Seán, you don't seem to do what we want on this course. You seem to do your own thing and follow your own path. I don't think you're going to make it through the course. In fact, I don't think you're going to make it as a journalist. If I were you, I would think of doing something different.'

And that was it. My life's dream and vocation were shattered in under 15 seconds by a man who had hard grey eyes and a jacket with elbow patches and who used to stand and smoke a pipe while resting the outer side of his right hand shoe on his left knee. He may have stood oddly and been badly dressed, but I was shattered. Utterly shattered. It was as if I had spent years chipping out and digging a vital path through a challenging mountain range only for his comments to bring, in a few seconds, all my hopes crashing down in an avalanche, blocking that hard earned path to fulfilment.

I realised I had two choices: Option 1 was to accept what he said and, complete with shattered confidence and belief, seek a safer, duller and less challenging and therefore less rewarding life. Option 2 was to realise that the man was clearly insane and talking utter rubbish and thus fight against such devastatingly negative claptrap and go and prove him wrong.

I took Option 2. I completed the course. I still did my own thing as I didn't really care for some of the samey writing styles they tried to instil in us and I went on to pass the course and 'qualify' as a journalist. The irony is that you only really learn about journalism when you're working in the thick of it, after training. A mainly classroom-based course doesn't and can't teach you to deal with seeing the badly charred remains of a four-year-old girl who died in a house fire, or various human body parts following an explosion, or being held at gunpoint by a meathead soldier in a war-ravaged country – all of which I experienced, along with many other testing episodes.

In fact, I also didn't care for another lecturer on the course who used to plonk his round and bursting frame down at the teacher's desk and then promptly disappear behind the broadsheet local newspaper which he read in between bursts of talking at us from behind it while repeating, almost word for word, what was in our course workbook. One day I just slipped out of class without him noticing and went to work on it from my college room as I could read it for myself a lot more interestingly. I got a good pass.

A few years later, I went back to the college to see one of my classmates who was doing a professional course that journalists had to do one and a half to two years after graduating from journalism college. As I passed my old classroom, the journalism lecturer who'd told me three years previously that I'd never make it on the course or in the profession, eagerly beckoned me in to meet the new intake of students.

He proudly introduced me as a 'shining example' of what one of his students could achieve – I had by then, aged 21, become the youngest network TV news correspondent the UK had ever had – and he made much of this chance encounter. He asked me to give an off-the-cuff inspirational talk on life after journalism college. I duly obliged.

I remember telling them with great relish (and truth) that if they wanted to get on in their chosen profession that they should remember two things: one, that they should believe in themselves and not be afraid to believe in themselves; and, two, that if they wanted to get on in the challenging but exciting world of journalism that they 'should ignore everything that people like him (at this point I pointed at my former lecturer) tell you!'

I'll never forget the look on his face that morning. The students loved it and laughed about my being so cheeky. I hope they heeded my advice, certainly when I explained what he had told me on that Monday afternoon about three years previously. So, belief is important and will help you achieve confidence and reinforce it.

Acceptance

We would all find it much easier to feel more self-confident if we'd only accept who we are as a whole. We spend too much time worrying about what other people think about us rather than focusing on what we think of ourselves because the latter is what should drive the way we live. We spend far too much time focusing on how much everyone else has or is going to have, a subject on which we could win Mastermind, if comparing yourself to other people were our specialist subject on the BBC TV quiz programme.

Research has shown that 50% of our emotional make-up is genetic, 10% is due to general circumstances like our education, our income and whether we're married or single, and the remaining 40% is down to our individual behaviour and approach to what life throws at us.[4]

This means that we shape almost half of our psyche and therefore how we view ourselves in that context is for us to mould. Even if you've had bad experiences in early and/or later life, or are even having them at the moment, you must see the greater picture. We are all as unique as we are fallible. Even the seemingly most gifted people have their weak points and, likewise, we all have our strong points. We all have talents. It's just a matter of discovering what those talents and strong points are and then fine tuning them.

It's the same with genetics. Some people are born more physically attractive than others. But it doesn't mean they're sexy or attractive as a whole. In fact, some of the most physically beautiful women, who are clever and much admired, can be some of the most screwed-up and unhappy people who can't accept who they are. And yet, to look at them and the lives you believe they have, you would think that they would want for nothing. Not so. And yet there are men and women who may not have the front cover features of their better looking peers, but they have an attitude and energy that makes them more attractive and sexier.

The most attractive people you will come across all have a greater air of warm and engaging reconciliation about them. They appear very natural – and naturalness is one of the first victims of our society as so many of us spend far too much time trying to be something we think other people want, hope or expect us to be rather than being as real on the inside as we are on the outside.

REAL LIFE STORY

Sir Ranulph Fiennes is described by the *Guinness Book of World Records* as the world's greatest living explorer. The British adventurer holds several endurance records. The former member of the SAS has undertaken numerous expeditions and was the first person to visit both the North and South Poles by surface means and the first to completely cross Antarctica on foot. In May 2009, at the age of 65, he climbed to the summit of Mount Everest.

And yet, when he was younger, he wanted to commit suicide because he hated himself and his life so much.

After two years at the famous British private school Eton and after being given a tough time for being a 'pretty boy', he 'strenuously thought about committing suicide by jumping off Windsor Bridge which would have been handy,' said Sir Ranulph.

He then took up boxing which he thought would make him less pretty. He did well and joined the school boxing team and also did night building climbing.

'I have never been introspective or philosophical and if I suddenly realise I might be feeling depressed I order myself to stop feeling depressed, pointing out that it is pointless. I also point out that one will be dead pretty soon, one way or another, and one might as well not spend time being despondent. So, when things are going badly, keep attacking.

'If, for instance, you're not getting any money for an expedition you've got to attack all that bit harder – be on the phone to more people, think of new ways of doing it. You could say that confidence is thinking that, sooner or later, your luck will turn and things will go right. And remember, you're always much better off than thousands of other people.'

In 1992 Fiennes led an expedition that discovered the lost city of Ubar in Oman. The following year he joined nutrition specialist Dr Mike Stroud in an attempt to become the first to cross the entire Antarctic Continent without support. Having crossed the continent in 90 days, they were forced to call for a pick-up on the Ross Ice Shelf, frostbitten and starving, on day 95. An attempt in 1996 ended in failure when he developed kidney stones halfway there.

In 2000, Sir Ranulph attempted to walk solo and unsupported to the North Pole. The expedition failed when his sleds fell through weak ice and Fiennes had to pull them out by hand. He sustained severe frostbite to the tips of all the fingers on his left hand, forcing him to abandon the attempt. On returning home, his surgeon insisted the necrotic fingertips be retained for several months (to allow regrowth of the remaining healthy tissue) before amputation. Impatient at the pain the dying fingertips caused, Fiennes attempted to remove them himself in his garden shed with a fretsaw. When this didn't work he picked up a Black & Decker in the nearby village with a micro blade and cut them off just above the blood and soreness.

Despite suffering from a heart attack and undergoing a double heart bypass operation just four months before, Fiennes joined Stroud again in 2003 to carry out the extraordinary feat of completing seven marathons in seven days on seven continents. 'In retrospect I wouldn't have done it. I wouldn't do it again. It was Mike Stroud's idea,' he later remarked.

In 2007, despite weakness from vertigo, he climbed the notorious North Face of the Eiger. And on 20 May 2009, Fiennes successfully reached the summit of Mount Everest, becoming the oldest British person to achieve this.

'No matter how weedy you are or whether you are too fat there are always a greater number of people who are worse off than you are and there are always people who are better off than you are. So you can spend time looking at either group and either be grateful that you're not like the former group or work harder to become like the latter.'

REAL LIFE STORY

One of the best real life examples of self-acceptance was told to me by the famous spy novelist and former British Cold War spy John le Carré. He had once come across an undercover US Drug Enforcement Agency (DEA) agent who pulled off an audacious undercover sting operation that netted a lot of major drug barons.

The agent's cover was that of a pimp and he got to know and charm all the main players, so much so that they all agreed to come to a large dinner held in their honour. Once his guests had settled into the dinner the agent stood up to make a speech. He made everyone laugh and had the audience in the palm of his hand. They laughed even louder when he told them with mock irony that they were all under arrest and they were splitting their sides when he added, laughing himself, that they were surrounded and should stick their hands up. Seconds later, DEA agents stormed the building from all quarters and arrested the drug bosses and their associates.

The undercover agent had spent months having to watch his every move, his every word and his every thought. Even one simple mistake could have exposed his true identity and put him at risk of a hideous death. Interestingly, said le Carré, the only people who had wondered about him were the prostitutes he had pimped. Unlike the other pimps, he never physically abused them, which they thought was odd, but reassuring.

This agent, a big, warm and brave man, was what le Carré described, with heartfelt intensity, as 'someone who was reconciled', someone who had accepted himself completely, who had accepted his role in life and the fact that he might die – and that helped him pull off this daring undercover sting.

The more accepting you are of yourself the more you appear to be at peace with yourself and the world. And that is something people find very attractive because you come across as soothing, selfless, supportive, stable and, where applicable, even sensual.

Persistence

As the 30th President of the USA Calvin Coolidge said, 'Nothing in the world can take the place of persistence. Talent will not; nothing is more common than unsuccessful men with talent. Genius will not; unrewarded genius is almost a proverb. Education will not; the world is full of educated derelicts. Persistence and determination alone are omnipotent. The slogan 'Press On' has solved and always will solve the problems of the human race.'

Some of the greatest inventions and actions have been the result of persistence. Persistence is the ability to maintain your momentum regardless of your feelings, your faults and your failures. It's about pressing on even – in fact, particularly – when you feel like giving up.

Persistence forces us to keep pressing on so we will at least achieve something rather than those prematurely weary and weak souls who give up too early and achieve nothing and, as a result, have to live with the quiet torment of their weakness.

REAL LIFE STORY

The designer of the iconic Dyson bagless vacuum cleaner, Sir James Dyson, took 15 years of frustration and 5,127 failed prototypes to perfect his bagless vacuum cleaner technology. His wife, an art teacher, helped support them both financially as best she could. There were countless times when he wanted to give up.

He's now a billionaire and is still persisting with perfecting his products and his business and expanding it for the benefit of his customers across the world and for those he works with.

Sir James said: 'The odds are against inventors when they first start out. Invention requires risks. You often don't know how long it will take to turn a concept into something that works. Then you need to spend considerable time and money getting it off the ground. I spent five years developing my vacuum cleaner and about 15 more trying to get it made. I had to put my house on the line to secure a loan. Of course you have doubts and worries about these decisions, especially when you have a young family, as I did. It's difficult when money is just going out but not coming in. But they gave me a lot of support because they saw I believed in the idea. If you have faith in invention, others will too. And that's what gets you through the hard times.

'The trick I used was not to be afraid of failure but to embrace it. To me as an inventor, each of the 5,000 prototypes I made was a failure in some way. I learned this from Jeremy Fry, who ran Rotork. He was my mentor and taught me how to design iteratively. Rather than going back to the drawing board, each time, by making small changes, I could learn from my mistakes and make improvements. Failure became a process, not a barrier. Of course it can become frustrating and you start to wonder if you're making any headway. But then I'd just compare my first prototype, a cardboard cyclone stuck to an old vacuum cleaner, with the latest iteration. Seeing the progress was a motivator.

'I suppose you develop a sense of cussedness as an inventor that pushes you forward. If you look at someone like Frank Whittle, he came from a working-class background and developed the jet engine while he was training to be an officer. Not your typical academic background but he had something more important: character. You need to be stubborn to be able to keep going and turn a good idea into something tangible. When I was trying to sell my vacuum cleaner to the multinationals having such an attitude meant I wouldn't give away my idea for a meagre royalty. It meant that I would end up manufacturing them myself. Jeremy Fry told me once: never trust an expert. Sometimes you have to go with your gut. If you know you have a good idea you have to pursue it.

'I wanted to give up almost every day. But one of the things I did when I was young was long distance running, from a mile up to 10 miles. They wouldn't let me run more than 10 miles at school – in those days they thought you'd drop down dead or something. And I was quite good at it, not because I was physically good, but because I had more determination. I learned determination from it.

'A lot of people give up when the world seems to be against them, but that's the point when you should push a little harder. I use the analogy of running a race. It seems as though you can't carry on, but if you just get through the pain barrier, you'll see the end and be okay. Often, just around the corner is where the solution will happen.'

But you can and will achieve what you want without having to make a world famous invention or perform a publicly recognised deed. This happens every day and could happen more often if only people were more determined to persist, enabling them to accomplish at least some small and worthwhile achievements. Persistence invariably does achieve results, whether you are famous or not, as I found out when I was a TV news correspondent. This next story still moves me now.

REAL LIFE STORY

One day, when sitting in the newsroom, I received a telephone call from a slightly shy sounding man. He felt nervous calling a television newsroom – mind you, who wouldn't, because if he'd actually been to such a snake pit then he definitely wouldn't have called – and was almost apologetic for suggesting he might have a potential story for me. Newsrooms field a lot of calls from members of the public and PR professionals hoping to get publicity for one thing or another, and too often they're either dull or ridiculous.

He stuttered his way through the first minute of our conversation, muttering something about a machine to help his daughter. It didn't sound particularly exciting, but something told me to stick with it and to find out more. I felt sorry for him as he sounded in awe of the situation and felt awkward about having to make a call asking for help. When I asked a few more questions, the story became clearer.

His daughter was extremely ill suffering from a debilitating disease which left her bed-ridden and unable to help or even express herself. Everything, like feeding her and taking her to the loo, had to be done by this man and his wife. The problem was that they would have to send her to a specialist unit a long way from their home in Cornwall because the specialist machine they had been relying on to feed her the necessary drugs and help her live was being taken away by the local health authority. But they wanted her to be at home with them, as did she.

The authority had told them that they could buy their own machine. But this was clearly out of the question as it cost far too much. And, as the father pointed out to me, 'We don't have much money. Well, certainly not now because it's all gone on helping our daughter.' They therefore couldn't afford to go on holidays or go out to dinner. They were loving slaves to their daughter's condition.

He asked if I could perhaps call up the local health authority as, being a TV news reporter, I might, as he put it, carry more weight than a member of the general public and might persuade them to reverse their decision. It was quiet in the newsroom, so I made the call and got a pleasantly detached press spokesman saying it was unfortunate, but that cost cutting meant that their 'hands are tied'. He also pointed out that there were others in a similar situation who would actually benefit from the withdrawal of the machines from their homes as the specialist care units they'd have to send the patients to now would make all their lives a lot easier. He had completely missed the point.

I called the father back and told him what they had said. He sounded disappointed and bade me a sad farewell, thanking me for my efforts. The next day he called me again and said that, after sleeping on the matter and discussing it with his wife and daughter, they would like me to do the story on them as it could only gain something for their daughter and, he said, for me as well. This humble sounding man was more resolute now and had thought about how it might benefit me, as well as his daughter. Although I didn't feel it was the strongest story around at that time, I sold it to the news editor and programme producers and went out to see how I could make this item come to life on TV.

As soon as I entered her bedroom and met all three of them, I could feel the tireless sense of dutiful care, diluted only slightly by the unspoken sorrow that they felt. I was incredibly moved and made the best of the story as I tastefully could. Although these filming sessions invariably have to stage different sequences to illustrate the story, I made sure the cameraman filmed them being as natural as possible, just letting them get on with caring for her as they always did.

The camera picked up the girl's expression which was frozen in sickly torment. She was almost unable to speak and yet her eyes stared directly and warmly at me and at the camera. I interviewed her father who came across as a deeply humble and caring individual but who, at the same time, was also quietly determined with a heart-touching dignity.

I made it back in time to get the story on the main lunchtime news. Two hours after it had been broadcast I received a call from him. He was almost in tears. 'I can't begin to thank you,' he said. 'People have been shoving £10 and £20 notes and cheques through the letterbox to help us buy a machine for our daughter so she can be treated at home and not be sent many miles away to a hospital in another part of the country. And that is down to you and the story you did on us.'

After the main evening programme piece went out, he received enough money to buy the machine to help him care for his daughter at home. When he called to tell me, I was almost in tears like he was.

Even though this man was initially in awe of the situation, feeling overpowered by the local authorities and circumstance, and also not feeling confident enough to contact the TV news station, he took action and tried something he probably thought would not work. He called up a TV newsroom in the seemingly vain hope that we might have been able to do something. And after the initial call I made on his behalf didn't work, he didn't give up there. He reappraised his approach and thought how he could persuade me, which he did, and it was this movingly humble persistence which led to me covering the story and him getting even more than he could have dreamed of – for free.

Goal Plan

Having a goal or goals gives you a focus and to achieve them you need a plan. If you don't, as someone once said, it's like rushing to get in a taxi and then hurriedly and breathlessly telling the driver: 'Quick! Somewhere!' When you have direction in life then you have something to aim for. And you need to be specific. Saying you want to be rich is fine, but it's too general and unfocused. Saying you want, for instance, to earn a six-figure income in three years gives you something to plan and aim for.

When I was a boy, one of my dreams was to become a television and newspaper journalist. Aged 14, I decided that that was my vocation in life and I set about making it happen. I persuaded my local newspaper editor to let me write for them. So during my school holidays I would write under the guise of the *Malvern Gazette's* 'Village Voice!' I was paid 3.4p per line then. Luckily, things have improved since.

I pinpointed the reasons for this career choice after having an earlier and misguided urge to become a chartered accountant like my father. I realised by my early teens that there was more to being an accountant than a large office, with magnificent views, being the boss of a successful practice and having two or three secretaries instead of one like more normal senior accountants. Mathematics and I were never destined for a workable life together and the thought of audits and the dazzling array of tax complexities didn't exactly float my boat. Fair enough. Why, I asked myself, did I want to become a journalist – other than avoiding maths and tax audits?

I identified what I wanted out of life and therefore a career which would be central to most of my adult life. There were three reasons:

■ I was and still am fascinated by people.

■ I loved and still love writing.

■ I always wanted adventure.

Journalism and broadcasting were the obvious choice. So I set about formulating a plan of action as to how I was going to get what I wanted.

Throughout these years, I drew up a list of publications and stations I needed to find out more about and the people at those organisations who I needed to see. I read up what I could in the papers and other media to find out what was going on. I wanted to be ready for any opportunity within the profession.

Before leaving school I researched extensively all the journalism colleges and their courses to find out what I wanted to do and where I wanted to do it. I settled on what was then one of the country's top such institutions, in Cardiff in Wales. I found out exactly what was needed to gain entry and even what sort of tests and questions I was likely to have to deal with. I read a broadsheet newspaper and tabloid every day, jotting down key points and stories and waded my way through the *Encyclopaedia Britannica* just to make sure! I felt I knew everything that was going on and had gone on. I was a coiled spring of information.

When I sent in the application form for the course, along with a few thousand other aspiring young journalists, I was able to add about ten more pages than everyone else detailing the cuttings of the articles I had written, the work experience I had gained and other tangible forms of complete commitment to the Fourth Estate.

As I was embarking on such an important step in my career, I needed to build the very strongest foundation blocks to act as a strong and resilient platform from which to launch myself into my chosen vocation. I identified what I needed to know and planned who I needed to see, where they were and how I was going to grab their attention.

I prepared by researching and reading around my chosen subject so that even if I was over prepared, as in this case, all eventualities were covered from then on. This knowledge base gave me the confidence which, I hope, came across well at the subsequent interviews. I had put in a lot of planning and preparation because I was determined to impress my interviewers and make me stand out from the thousands of others I was competing against for a place. And I got it.

REAL LIFE STORY

Daisy Berkeley always had a goal of being the best in the world at equestrian events.

At the 2008 Olympic Games, after being called up at the last moment from the first team reserve, she won a team bronze medal. She also won the European team gold medal in the European Championships the year before and, in 2006, she won team silver at the World Championships. And Daisy, who graduated from Oxford University in 1993 after winning a 'blue' at lacrosse, finally won her first British Open eventing title at Gatcombe Park in 2010 on her horse 'Spring Along'.

'In my competition existence, confidence is very important because in my game you're trying to instil confidence in your horse, and if you're not riding in a confident fashion your horse won't feel like doing what you're asking it to. So I have to act in a confident way to have my horse's trust to make it do what I want it to do.

'Because I've been brought up with horses from a very young age (Daisy's father Dave Dick was a successful national hunt jockey who won the famous Grand National and the Gold Cup), I was always far more comfortable with horses and animals than I was with people. There is less pressure with animals.

'I'm much better with people now because success has brought confidence. I think this is something you find with people in sport; they're so focused on and obsessed with their sport they sometimes lose a bit on the social graces. But to survive in the world of sport, with the media, you have to develop confidence in that area. I was helped by doing a lot of drama at school, which helped me get through all that. But I had to develop it as I wasn't as confident as I was around animals.

'I used to have a problem with confidence because, as with most riders, there are very few people who go through their whole equestrian career riding good horses. Most of us have to do a bit of an apprenticeship riding yaks and camels! And I've had my fair share of yaks and camels! They give you bad experiences. They stop at the fences. They give you bad results. They give you a bad feeling riding them. They don't jump well. And the more a horse goes badly for you, the more you start to doubt yourself. It's only really good horses that make you start to actually believe in yourself.

'If I'm competing and have a big competition coming up I do a lot of mental visualisation techniques. I usually walk a course three or four times before I actually ride around it and, back in my horsebox or wherever I'm staying, I will actually shut my eyes and go through the course. And when I'm riding the course in my mind I'm perfect! I know exactly where I'm jumping it and sometimes I'll do different routes – Plan A and Plan B – and they're always very positive.

'Quite often, when you're lacking confidence, you will start to visualise yourself doing things wrongly. You get people walking courses and they cannot actually imagine being able to jump a particularly difficult fence successfully. You just have to mentally picture how you're going to do it and how you're going to do it properly. You can't expect to jump it in real life if you can't jump it in your mind.

'At the top level in my game you don't ride if you're frightened because that's actually very dangerous in itself. The only fear any of us would have is fear of failure.

'Overconfidence happened to me, particularly when I was a young rider in the under-21 age group. I rode a final trial for the young European Rider Championships and I was in the lead going into the cross-country. I had gone like the wind and I knew I was going to win it. I came up to the second to last fence, took a chance, because I was counting the money and planning my trip to Germany, on that occasion, and rode sufficiently badly at the fence that my horse never got a proper look at it. It did a summersault and we practically rolled through the finish line with the horse and I unattached!

'You have to put yourself in an environment where you can actually reach your goals or attempt to, even if you think you have any advantages. There are people in the equestrian world who have had it on a plate, but they're invariably not the ones who make it to the top. The ones who do make it to the top are the ones who have worked incredibly hard for it, base themselves with a real star of the sport and have worked from the bottom upwards. That way, they've done their initiation riding dodgy horses, taking the knocks, learning the hard way and so they've got the fight and the stomach to cope with it when they actually get to the top. You've got to fight your way to get there and it's never been plain sailing for anybody.

'I've had times when I was riding horrible horses I was so close to giving up, thinking 'what's the point?' There were people who I knew I was as good as who were getting up to the top and I thought I wasn't going to make it. But I kept fighting tooth and claw and finally managed to get my foot in the door. And then one good horse came my way and then, once I'd proved what I could do, then other good horses came my way. You need to prove to people that you're in there for the long haul and not just a flash in the pan.'

REAL LIFE STORY

Robert Clay is one of the world's leading marketers. He started his first business, aged 19, with no capital. In three years he achieved 40% penetration of his initial target market compared to the national average of 17% for all other brands combined. He built this business to be number three in the UK within seven years and franchised it worldwide.

At age 23 he invented the glass sunroof for cars, creating from scratch a market in the UK for more than 250,000 units a year within three years. It became the third largest sunroof manufacturer in Europe. Eventually he sold both businesses to one of the largest companies in

Europe and played a significant role in taking that business to number one in its field in the world within four years.

Since 1996 he has been accumulating, analysing and organising vast quantities of the world's most powerful marketing strategies and best practices into a vast interconnected map. That master map now contains over 435 million words, or some 1.8 million plus pages, and is still growing.

'I suppose the first time I spoke in public was nerve wracking, before the event. I prepared thoroughly, was in command of my subject matter and the talk went down very well with lots of great feedback. I then realised I had been worrying about nothing, decided just to be myself and in command of my subject matter and have never looked back since. The way I overcome lack of confidence is to be very thorough in preparing, so that I have all bases covered and then some,' said Robert.

'Because I am well prepared, I don't suffer from a lack of confidence. You could say it's down to sheer hard work and thoroughness.'

Self-confidence is life changing. It can and will enhance how you feel about yourself and therefore how people regard you and that, in turn, will boost your confidence further so that you become the confident person you've always wanted to be.

Chapter 2

What confidence can achieve

- GREATER HAPPINESS

- GREATER INNER PEACE

- GREATER EMOTIONAL SATISFACTION

- GREATER PROFESSIONAL OPPORTUNITIES

- GREATER FINANCIAL WEALTH

- GREATER COURAGE

- GREATER ADVENTURE

- GREATER LIFE OPPORTUNITIES

- GREATER INSPIRATION FOR OTHERS

Most of us believe that we're living our lives at about 50–75% of our potential. In other words, we're doing only half to three-quarters of the things we could be doing. In fact, I'll put it even more bluntly. The lives most of us are missing out on are the goals, hopes and desires that we REALLY want and need to make our existence more complete and worthwhile. And those are the aspects that require confidence, enabling us to have a go at achieving something which we can later look back on with contentment and, as a result, greater confidence.

It's much easier to take the less challenging option and live with that. But, in so many of us, there are niggling thoughts about what could be or even what might have been. This is down to a mixture of fear and lack of confidence. Whether it's bungee jumping from a perilous height, taking a spontaneous motorbike tour of Europe, asking that special person out on a date or leaving the job you've never really liked and starting your own business, most people take the safe option of maintaining the status quo.

Research has found that 75% of people, when looking back over their lives, regret not doing something while only 25% regret doing something.[5]

Doing the things that unnerve or even frighten you take you into the Adventure Zone – a mysterious, unpredictable and limitless place where anything can happen – where you have to address any lack of confidence as it's the only way to experience and enjoy all this environment has to offer. It's unsettling, but it can be excitingly life changing.

The other option is to stay in the Safe Zone – an easily identifiable, predictable and limited place where only certain things can happen – where limiting beliefs and limiting attitudes flourish with little risk of you benefitting from anything that might change your life for the better. It's the place to settle if you don't want to transform your life. The thing is most of us can and probably need to improve our lot – and instead a lot of us spend too much time wondering what life could be like if only we took that crucial step into the relatively unknown.

I know this from my personal and professional clients and from the seemingly endless number of people I meet who live as If Only people in the Safe Zone. If they have a certain level of life ambition, it doesn't really show. They exist with this manacle of often polite and restrained frustration because they haven't given this part of their life a proper go. This could be because they've been made to feel bad about themselves as a youngster, because they've never got the job or promotion they wanted, because they've got an overdraft, because their partner left them to marry a gnu called Bernard in the Far East, and a whole host of other random reasons.

Some or all of these things may well have happened – even if the gnu wasn't called Bernard – but that doesn't mean you have to be tied to that experience for the rest of your life and let it flavour and dominate how you live your life, particularly if it doesn't make you feel good. When I was a young boy, my school barber used to give me a fringe – a huge haircut no-no. I had to live with it then, and now, not having enough hair to even use as a crime scene hair sample, let alone to cut a fringe. I have to say that it has never stopped me!

So, would you swim with jellyfish if you knew they would sting you? If you have to think about that for even a second, then Bernard beckons as does some bizarre ensuing marriage ceremony. Wouldn't you go and find somewhere else for sting-free and limb and life damaging-free swimming? And in doing so you will more than likely have to explore new places and options which in turn will give you a new perspective. And you'd also be more thorough about finding out how safe the water was to swim in. You'd do more, gain more and feel more in control because you developed the courage to take the action you needed to achieve what you wanted. You'd make things happen and develop the level of confidence you may well have been lacking.

Confidence gives you the impetus and therefore the self-belief to grasp opportunities in life so you can enjoy them and even succeed where you might not have otherwise. Therefore you can find new and deeper ways of fulfilling your potential to achieve happiness, success and stronger self-esteem. And if you are married to a gnu called Bernard, then good for you for giving it a go with a rather dysfunctional and hysterical migrating wildebeest … as that takes confidence.

REAL LIFE STORY

Rachel Elnaugh made millions of pounds and then lost it and had to start again. She's the entrepreneur who created the market-leading experiences brand Red Letter Days at the age of 24. She grew it from nothing, on a shoestring budget, into a household name with a multi-million pound turnover. This won her an Ernst & Young Entrepreneur of the Year Award in 2002 and, as a result, she became one of the 'Dragons' in the BBC TV series 'Dragons' Den'. But, in 2005, Red Letter Days fell into administration.

She later wrote about her experiences of adversity in business in her 2007 book *Business Nightmares*. Rachel has been an Entrepreneur in Residence at the British Library Business and IP Centre since 2008 and gives free monthly mentoring sessions to entrepreneurs. She now speaks about enterprise and her experiences.

'Confidence is important, particularly in business because you're constantly having to go out there, put yourself at the front of your business, doing the deals, making the calls, being the figurehead and being the front person. And unless you've got the confidence to be able to go out and lead, life is very difficult.

'When I was young I used to feel very ugly and not liked and not wanted. But I was always prepared to get up and try things and I was prepared to make a fool of myself. Thinking back to my childhood, there were two incidents. One was when I was involved in this amateur dramatic society and I was understudying one of the lead characters. And one day she didn't turn up and I had to go and do this part. I was so young and I hadn't prepared for it and I just ran away and hid, in the toilets somewhere, because I just couldn't face it. And I think that really broke my confidence a lot.

'That terror of performing and being put in the spotlight is something I've had to face in my adult life. I also remember doing a public speaking event at school when I was voted best speaker. I took a chance and did it on a completely off the wall topic and won great applause for that. So I had a very mixed experience of success and failure. In terms of putting yourself out there, sometimes it can go brilliantly and sometimes it can go horribly wrong.

'When I started Red Letter Days I'd just been working in the City. I was working for Arthur Andersen and I had quite a high-flying career. So when I went into business I was full of confidence because I felt I knew it all and I thought it would be so easy, like turning on a tap. And I very quickly realised, within weeks, that it was going to be really, really tough because when you're within an organisation which has got loads of respect you automatically get that respect, whereas when you're starting up from scratch, particularly with a concept that no one's heard of, and you're 24 and you're female, it's really difficult to even get people to talk to you, let alone take you seriously.

'And so I went through a really gruelling 18 months of nothing working and that was a really, really tough period. I think that was my trial by fire of entrepreneurship. If you can survive that pit at the start-up stage where just nothing's working, no one's taking your calls, cash isn't flowing, I think you can probably survive anything.

'Red Letter Days had grown. We'd had over a decade of great growth. We were profitable and we were making a million pound profit a year. I was winning awards. I had been invited to go on the telly and all that kind of great stuff. But actually I was then experiencing the other side, that overconfidence where you suddenly think you've got the Midas touch and you can take over the world. So we then went on this huge growth campaign. We were thinking let's float on AIM, let's drive turnover. And actually that was our downfall to really drive the business too hard and too fast. Overconfidence, really.

'It led to the business, within 18 months, going from that million pound profit to plunging to a £4.7 million loss which was a disaster and really difficult to recover from. Although I spent two and a half years trying to recover from it, we were finally forced into administration by our bank in 2005. It was the end of a 16-year journey – a roller coaster ride of great highs and great lows'.

Post-Red Letter Days: 'I actually needed the money, but I was terrified of public speaking. So for me to put myself out there on the stage, having actually wanted to stay at home with the curtains shut, but knowing I had to do it was quite something for me. I actually forced myself to face that fear. And I kind of got through, probably with the first 50 gigs, and then I had this flip where I actually thought this is a real privilege and I'm going to make myself good at it. So then I started enrolling a vocal coach and a presentation trainer and all that stuff. And I'm still working on that, but 300 gigs later I now feel I'm starting to master being able to do great speaking events.

'You can face your fear. I remember one event where there were 300 top entrepreneurs in the audience. I was coming in from the back as the first speaker on and I was terrified. I wanted to jump out of the toilet window. But on occasions like that you've just got to find it in you to push through that fear and turn the nerves into something more positive.

Being a woman in business is always a double-edged sword because, on one hand, I wasn't taken seriously and so people wouldn't take my calls, I couldn't get meetings with people, but, on the other hand, I did ask for help. And what I found was that people took me under their wing and, as a woman, you've got that ability for people to feel sorry for you and to take pity on you and help you. And I found a great mentor and marketer in the beginning who really helped me to get the business right and find that formula. When you get the formula right in business, it's amazing how quickly it takes off. You could be struggling for a long time before you get it right.

'With this guy's help, suddenly the business went from nothing to taking off overnight. Interestingly, then, all the people who wouldn't talk to me in the early days were knocking on my door. It was very tempting to say, "No, actually, I don't want to deal with you now!" But you just forgive them and move on.

'It's very easy, isn't it, to find all the reasons why not; all the blocks: "I can't afford it", "I'm not pretty enough" and "I'm not good at speaking." I ask entrepreneurs I mentor, who come out with those blocks, if they had to find a way, what would they do? There is always a way if you want to achieve something. All those things are just artificial limiting beliefs that just get in the way. I'm a great believer in having that mindset of "I can" and then finding a way.'

Below are some examples of just some of the things that clients, friends and others – and even you – want to achieve and, with the right encouragement, will and have gone on to realise:

- Really like yourself

- Find a great partner or spouse who you thought was 'out of your league'

- Make more money

- Improve your (existing) relationship with your partner or spouse

- Seek some better friends and acquaintances

- Dump certain people from your social circle

- Improve your sex life

- Find more sexual partners

- Need fewer sexual partners

- Join a nunnery or monastery

- Enjoy greater inner peace

- Go for a better job

- Give up your job

- Start your own business

- Go on a life-changing adventure

- Run for public office

- Tell people what you really think

- Leave the country

- Feel more physically attractive

- Lose weight

- Be less fearful

- Be unafraid of failing

- Speak confidently in public

- Do something daring like a bungee jump or a parachute jump

- Join a Special Forces unit

- Laugh more

- Lead a less stressful life

The thing is that self-confidence is achievable. But despite this so many of us falter and choose to believe we are not confident. This book will show you everything you need to know to make you more confident in a practical and practicable way. It will induce you to be honest with yourself and examine what your fears are and how to overcome them. And it will, above all else, help you realise what your strengths are and how to capitalise on them, whether professionally, socially, emotionally, financially, physically or even sexually.

REAL LIFE STORY

While serving in the Vietnam War, Jim Stevens was shot in the head by an enemy soldier. Doctors couldn't remove the bullet and, for the next 20 years, he had severe, recurring migraines.

In 1994, a particularly painful migraine triggered a stroke and Jim lost all but 2% of his vision. He was angry. He lost his eyesight and his job and his wife left him. This made him a blind man with two young daughters to bring up. One day, in a fit of rage, he destroyed much of his unfinished art pieces and notes.

In time, he opened up about his feelings to his youngest daughter who convinced him he was still needed. 'That broke my heart and finally got my attention,' said Jim.

'For six years I felt that I couldn't do anything, let alone anything right,' said Jim. But then things changed.

'In 2000, I met a gruff and unsympathetic martial arts instructor who convinced me to study Kenpo Karate even though I was legally blind. After a year of study, I began to realise that if I could do this there had to be other possibilities beyond my disability. I slowly began to believe in myself again and I repaired my destroyed art studio and began to work on my art again using several different visual lenses to help me see the art I was trying to work on.'

Years ago, when he was deeply frustrated with his situation, Jim could have quit.

'After years of struggle, I finally re-mastered my skills and the quality of my art. Today my work is collected internationally, I am the author of three books on the art of American scrimshaw, my work is in art galleries across the country and I was recently honoured as a Kennedy Center VSA Registered Artist in both the visual and literary arts.'

After four years, Jim earned a black belt. Today, he is the only legally blind man to win the Martial Arts Tournament of Champions men's fighting competition. He says spectators were unaware of his blindness. He is also the only blind man to be honoured as a Kenpo Shodan – a Shaolin Black Belt.

'Though it was a certainly a struggle at times, today I believe in myself again. I lost everything. But today I am a respected and successful artist and author with a new philosophy. The only real guarantee in life is change and I have learned to embrace change. I believe in placing my confidence and hope in the uncertainty of change. We all experience change, for better or for worse. It is the confidence we have within us that allows us to overcome those changes with dignity and success,' added Jim.

Chapter 3

What affects our confidence

The main factors that affect our confidence are:

- ■ PARENTS AND FAMILY

- ■ SCHOOL

- ■ THE MEDIA

- ■ COLLEAGUES

It's useful to understand how and why your confidence is affected because it will give you a useful context and perspective to help you find, build and sustain confidence in a more powerful way.

Fear is the main underlying factor in a lack of confidence and it is affected principally by one of the four aspects listed above and detailed in this section. More than half the people in my survey admitted that, in order of significance, fear of failure, fear of the unknown and fear of embarrassment were the three things that stopped them from being more confident. And these can be very overwhelming and set a damaging precedent for life.

That's why this book will help you understand and overcome your fears and afflicted levels of confidence, no matter how they have been ground down. Because if you can gain greater understanding of what has caused your lack of confidence generally, or in a specific area of your life, then you can find a way to counter that influence, no matter how excruciating or embarrassing.

Parents and family

Your upbringing helps form the basis of the person you turn out to be. As mentioned above, research has shown that almost 50% of who we are is down to our genetic make-up. The remainder of how we feel, think and react to things that happen to us and to others is based on our experiences and, more importantly, how we deal with them.

So, if your mother or father never quite got the hang of parenting and couldn't work out what to do with you from the moment you were born, then this could have an unhealthy influence on your development. I'm often amazed at how parents behave with their children and what they say to them.

I remember going to an English country wedding of a female barrister where the father of the bride greeted me at the post-ceremony, pre-reception line-up with intense and almost theatrical joy and told me, with many others listening, that his daughter wasn't much of a looker, but had one or two good points. His daughter was in fact very clever, calm, kind, warm and a successful young barrister – amazing, considering the seemingly proud father thought of her as a Plain Jane. From what I knew of her, she was marrying a very lucky man.

REAL LIFE STORY

Some parents' behaviour with their children can be counter-productive. Lisa, who's now 46 years old, hasn't really succeeded in her business ventures and always had problems when growing up.

'I always struggled at school, being a perfectionist, and failed much of the time. Unfortunately, my mother also lived in denial and kept reasserting my excellent performance in school, which was not the case. My potential did not match the reality. This is where being scrupulously honest will assist me, in terms of charting a path and following it,' said Lisa.

She added: 'I would say to someone who lacks self-confidence: Your life will change and things will move in your favour when you pick your head up off the floor. No one will do it for you, and that may not feel fair, but you will feel very proud of yourself for seeking help and guidance and you will gain dignity and self-respect in the process.'

At the extreme end of the scale, some so-called parents have been allowed to produce children they then neglect or even abuse. At best, they will give their offspring a substandard form of parenting in between bouts of boozing, fighting and following a variety of careless habits that give the worst example to their children who then often replicate this destructive blueprint of behaviour. A great risk then follows that they will grow up with the same attitude and pursue the same dangerously wasteful life.

I have worked with kids from the roughest end of the social spectrum who, as teenagers, and even younger, have been involved with guns and drugs and taken part in armed robberies, knife attacks, assault and general violence. I have seen the homes they were growing up in and met the parents or step-parents or, in many cases, the lovers and passing others who sometimes tried but often failed to fulfil, permanently or fleetingly, the parental guidance role. And it's frightening. No wonder some of these once impressionable children grow up into the scourge of our society and seek a misaligned confidence through crime and gang culture.

At the other end of the social spectrum, I have seen how children of some of the wealthy and socially well placed are treated as culturally and socially expected accessories. It's almost as if they are bred because that's what society expects of certain parents and not necessarily because the children are desired for their own sake.

You can tell by the way certain parents – particularly the emotionally controlled ones – react to little Cuthbert. As soon as he can string a parentally pleasing sentence together in the Queen's English he is then dispatched to boarding school. This leaves the parents to go and get on with their lives. And of course there's nothing little eight-year-old Cuthbert likes more, when he finally gets to see his parents after weeks or longer without their love and support being physically available to him, than a good, firm handshake from the pater. That could almost be emotionally nourishing. Why hug and kiss him lovingly when other parents and people might be watching who would think it was all a bit much and a little too emotionally expressive.

So it doesn't matter what part of the social spectrum you come from, your parents' behavioural traits can and will affect you. Your confidence can so easily be undermined because that's when you're at your most vulnerable. This is because it's a child's instinct to look up to their parents as the trusted source of learning about life and about how they should be in the world. Siblings, certainly elder ones, can also have a good or bad effect on you.

School

School can sometimes make you or break you. With great and inspiring teachers you are more likely to enjoy a subject and want to learn more. You can also make lifelong friends. But sadly there are teachers who obviously learn their craft from some mean-spirited tinpot dictator with some spare time on his hands to teach the finer points of mental and physical torment. Such people can undermine not only your love for and even ability in a given subject, but can also instil in you a most affecting lack of confidence.

One such person in my childhood was a former Spanish teacher. I loved the language as my mother speaks it fluently and I found it easier to learn than French. Unfortunately my teacher was a deranged and cussed Scotsman who disliked schoolboys and, we suspected, mankind. For, if we got anything wrong when he demanded we answer a question in Spanish, he would make us kneel on pencils. That hurts. After two or three minutes, it's agony.

I didn't mind the fact that he always wore the same old ill-fitting sports jacket, with elbow patches, that was a walking DNA database of his life and lunches from the past 60 years. I didn't even mind the fact that his mouth was a jumbled junk yard of browned and irregular teeth. All I wanted was for him to teach us a really useful language rather than use it as a front to verbally and physically torment boys in their early teens.

And there were others: from the six foot tall male science teacher who punched me so hard in the solar plexus, when as a ten year old I had been wisecracking in the school laboratory, that I stopped breathing and didn't get up from the ground for three minutes, to the headmaster who liked thrashing pre-teenage boys with an assortment of canes, sometimes until the said boys' buttocks bled. These sorts of experiences are not good for morale. They're not only unreassuring, but also potentially undermining.

Although I had a few really good teachers throughout my school career, I also had a series of teachers who, despite my parents' hopes and initial belief that they would guide me on to greatness in life, told me I was at best just average academically and that I wasn't going to achieve much. With one or two rare exceptions, not once did they see or bring out the skills I have used to succeed in life where they said I would fail.

All that can really undermine your confidence and can and will create problems for you as you try to make your way in the world. With me, it made me all the more determined to rely on myself, as I couldn't rely on my teachers or my school, for the most part, as I wanted to prove that their negative thinking was wrong and that I could and, as it turned out, did achieve what I wanted to in life.

REAL LIFE STORY

Rob is now a successful entrepreneur who had a dysfunctional school and home life. His father, a former Royal Marines Commando, was a heroin addict and dealer who spent much of Rob's early life 'at Her Majesty's pleasure'.

'I grew up in a house with no internal doors because my father had sold them for drugs. I was a free school meals kid. I went to an academically terrible comprehensive school in the North of England graduating with seven O-levels and a GCSE grade 4 in Art. I was expelled during my A-levels and after spending a year being unemployed and having a spread of crap jobs I retook my A-levels at the same college, but only after some considerable negotiation with the college to allow me back!' said Rob.

Despite this awful educational start, he now has three businesses focusing on different areas of market research, and has already sold a fourth. He now earns a healthy six-figure income.

Your fellow pupils can also affect your confidence. Kids can bully you for a wide variety of things. You can get picked on and tormented for being ugly, good looking, thick, clever, red headed, short, fat, talented, richer, poorer, having embarrassing parents, shy, physically deformed or disabled and so on and so forth. Children can be as cruel as they can be charming.

One of the boys in the same year at my first boarding school was picked on quite quickly. I can't remember why exactly. We were only eight years old. But he did possess a physical oddity that caught people's attention. The end of his penis had a kink in it so it was more L-shaped than I-shaped. That mustn't have helped matters, certainly as he had to stand at a tricky angle when going for a pee to make sure he didn't 'misfire'.

I used to get woken up in the middle of the night by his crying after a few of the other boys had leapt onto his bed and hit him. He was the fastest boy in our year and a very talented sprinter. He had a great sporting future ahead of him and, ironically, when we arrived nervously on that first day, he was the most at ease and confident among us. But all that changed.

Tragically, as the teasing and bullying went on through our five years at this geographically remote school, he developed a stutter and a most noticeable twitch where he would jut his head forward like a chicken. That made matters worse and he withdrew into himself an even more broken person whose confidence had been ripped from him during what had been a torrid time. He stopped competing and I never saw his sporting prowess displayed again.

Once in a while I wonder what happened to him. I hope he is a happier man now and enjoys the success he should have been able to enjoy at school if only his confidence hadn't literally been beaten out of him.

The media

The media is a wonderful source of mind-stretching information, ranging from the beastly and beautiful to the bizarre and baffling. And although there are many stories out there that make us feel lucky to have the life we do, there are also many that make us question what we possess and who we are.

The latter can make us feel inadequate and as if we're not earning enough, good looking enough, have enough friends or having enough limb-quivering sex. In fact I'm not sure if you've ever had limb-quivering sex – so much better when no one's filming you – but there can be a tendency to expect it morning, noon and night if some magazines (not ones like *Chemical Engineering Weekly, Corporation Tax Monthly* or *Ostrich News* … we hope), tabloid newspapers and more off the wall TV shows (not BBC TV's 'Songs of Praise', I believe) will have you believe.

In certain glossy and other magazines of a similar neurosis-inducing ilk, as well as tabloid newspapers, we are invariably drenched in often unattainable sights and thoughts of female beauty, poise and wondrous lifestyles. It's a very clever way of making the often unrealistic appear realistic. And once the initial excitement of the potential for personal perfection has dissipated and the feverishly worshipped image of the new you has been diluted by the reality of your bottom, breasts or other bits which you feel don't quite measure up (even though, in reality, you probably have nothing to worry about), it's very easy to feel less confident about yourself. Comparison can corrode confidence as quickly as you can flick through rows of glossy magazine pages.

Interestingly, research has shown that two-thirds of women find fault with their bodies, even if this is unjustified, whereas two-thirds of men like their bodies, even if this is unjustified.

But we live in an age where, increasingly, men cannot afford to take for granted that they can be naturally attractive to women without making an effort to look after themselves. As women now have a greater independence and therefore a reduced dependence on men in many areas of life, they can be and are more choosy. Men can no longer assume that women will be looking for and depending on the male of the species to bring them emotional, social, financial, professional and sexual salvation.

For the most part, women are increasingly on roughly the same playing field in life as men and with roughly the same rules. Therefore, for instance, men cannot leave it only to the women to be waxed, blow-dried and plucked to make them more appealing only for men not to make a parallel effort themselves. And the media reflects and accentuates this.

That's why men face a similar set of issues through the male orientated side of this kind of media. Read any tabloid newspaper about how some very accommodating woman has managed to make sure she slept with someone famous – I'm sure to make him feel loved and desired and not, of course, to further her 'career' as a 'singer' – and you get a variety of headlines and subheadings. These include words and phrases like 'gasp', 'insatiable', 'hunk', 'well endowed', 'wealthy' and 'successful'. These send out subliminal messages to men that they have got to be at least two hours and eight inches long with the looks and the loot to lure 'pulsating lovelies'.

Needless to say, it's very easy to feel you don't measure up and that everyone else has much more than you because the media is very good at dressing up the mundane to appear magnificent and selling an intoxicatingly intriguing utopian view of life as it is and could be.

Colleagues

Like family, you can't always choose your work colleagues unless you're the boss and it's your own business. Your colleagues are like your daytime-cum-working hours family. They can be supportive and fun. They can also be difficult and debilitating on both a professional and personal level.

Depending on the work environment and the type of business you're in, you're going to see your colleagues at their best and at their worst and they will be able to see you in the same way too. This can make you very close, leading to great friendships, work romances, embarrassing and awkward primeval urges and, once you have got through that, even marriage. No wonder that 55% of office romances lead to marriage.[6] But it can also make you dislike or even detest your colleagues and vice-versa.

If you don't hit it off with someone and it gets out of hand then the situation can get very stressful and undermine your confidence. Bullying in the workplace is an issue, no matter how much the 'we're part of a family here' mantra is wafted around from the senior management to the sometimes disbelieving ranks of their staff.

One of the great things about becoming an adult, or so we believe, is that we don't have to suffer in our adult lives the same sort of classroom or playground politics that causes many a lot of anguish throughout our youth. But that's not so. The only difference is that at least you get paid to sometimes endure the more advanced school playground and classroom environment that is the workplace. In the UK, for instance, research has shown that 18.9 million working days are lost each year as a direct result of workplace bullying. This is not helped by the fact that 43.5% of employers do not have a policy to deal with workplace bullying and that 93.1% of all human resources practitioners say that bullying is occurring in their own organisations.[7]

Bullying can come from your peers or a boss. Sadly, some of the people who not only work with others closely but, more frustratingly, are let loose on others to lead and manage them, are not great at dealing with people. It can be a vehicle for unleashing their peculiarities on others and using them as a psychological punchbag. This will undermine your confidence and therefore your performance if you're on the receiving end. This in turn will have an effect on you outside the workplace as what happens at home and at work are both interlinked. This can send you into a downward spiral of decreasing confidence and decreasing unhappiness, and so it goes on.

Your colleagues can of course become great mates. And we need a friendly working environment as we spend so much of our lives working to give us some purpose as well as money. But if a colleague is awful by being manipulative, back-stabbing, poisonously political or even physically aggressive, then this can be a corrosive experience that will devalue the days of your working week. Even the most confident of people will sometimes struggle if faced with such a hostile environment.

Humans, like most bits of highly tuned and complex machinery, are susceptible to malfunctions. We are vulnerable as much as we are capable. We quickly learn to adapt our behaviour to the limitations we feel or are made to feel because of what psychologists call 'learned helplessness'. This is a cause of negative and self-defeating behaviour.

But being able to develop and sustain an encouraging level of confidence will help you not only deal with such issues, it will also provide you with a strong base layer of belief.

Chapter 4

Overconfidence

Psychologists have found that overconfidence can make people overestimate their knowledge and underestimate risks. Overconfident people believe they are more able to succeed at something and therefore think they have a beneficial effect on events and people, when the complete antithesis can be true. While confidence enables us to grow and can also have a useful effect on others we deal with, overconfidence can produce the opposite effect.

You can be perceived as overconfident by someone who's intimidated by your in fact acceptable level of confidence, but that's more a case of how unconfident they are as opposed to you being overconfident. The contrast in attitude between you both, mixed with their self-perception of how unconfident they feel compared to the seemingly unattainable level of confidence you have, will give them this impression. It is no reflection on you or that you have an unwarranted belief in yourself.

But overconfidence is unhealthy in those who overestimate their abilities because they haven't developed a clear and wide ranging sense of awareness. One of the earliest pioneers of this sometimes baffling behavioural approach was the English King Canute. Flattered by his courtiers that he was so great that he could do anything, like stopping the waves, he sat in his throne at the seashore and ordered the waves to stop. Two wet feet and a dented regal ego later, he sloped off to take out his frustration in a punch-up with the Vikings.

Confidence is gained from trying things that we feel unable to do with consummate ease and where we have to use our various mental and physical resources to achieve what we want to. Overconfidence comes from when we feel we can deal with something that was once a challenge with little to no effort. And this can not only lead to mistakes being made, but also to your overconfidence being rapidly ripped back down to earth, along with your and other's hopes of succeeding at what you needed to.

I'll never forget a business pitch I was asked to be a part of years ago as a freelance TV producer. A contact had put me in touch with a man who ran his own small TV production company which had managed to get in to do a pitch with a highly successful entrepreneur's company for a good bit of business. He and I met up in a cafe nearby shortly before and went over our story and he talked me through how the meeting was going to go. He was very sure of himself. Hardly surprising as he was an eloquent, ambitious and good looking guy.

When, as devil's advocate, I pointed out some of the nastier questions this entrepreneur could ask us so we could prepare ourselves for such challenges, he dismissed them with a cocksure manner. He told me that the entrepreneur and his team were going to love the proposition, that he (my associate) was going to command the meeting – 'you just watch me deal with them,' he told me with great assurance – and that he could handle anything they threw at him.

The thing is that in the meeting itself they did throw things at him – all sorts of things – and he started to stumble and then crumble. It was excruciating. This wasn't helped by the fact that the man we were dealing with had a Zeppelin-sized ego and opinions and a voice to match. He was nothing short of rude within a couple of minutes of the meeting's start. Then, like a cat toying with its pitiful prey holding onto the last few seconds of its life, he ridiculed my colleague's proposition with excessive arrogance and vituperation so this previously overconfident man was left crushed and under confident.

I didn't hear from him after that and years later learnt that he had folded up the business and was working for someone else again.

More famous cases of overconfidence include the owners of the Titanic transatlantic liner who made people believe it was unsinkable. After it hit an iceberg, it sank in just over two hours killing more than 1,500 of the passengers on board.

The British government believed that their troops would all be home in time for Christmas in 1914 just months after they had gone to war with Germany, an equally mighty, but rearmed power. It was more than four years of The Great War and the needless deaths of millions before that could be realised.

The same could be said of more recent events like the Vietnam war and the wars in Iraq and Afghanistan which have been raging for far longer than they should have, costing the lives of thousands of men, women and children and all because the mighty powers believed they were greater than they actually were.

In 1999, researchers at Cornell University undertook an interesting study.[8] They found that most incompetent people have no idea they are incompetent and in fact have greater confidence in their abilities than much more capable people do in theirs. Their incompetents were blissfully ignorant of their shortcomings, grossly overestimated their abilities and were supremely self-assured despite there being no basis for it. Ignorance is bliss, as the saying goes, but not necessarily for those around the blissfully ignorant.

So, how do you combat overconfidence? If you are good or the best at something then, humans being human, there will be a day or days when, for a host of psychological and other reasons, some of them out of your control, you just don't operate as well as an overconfident person expects themselves to. So it's in our interests, no matter how capable we are, to try to get better and more consistently so we don't make the sort of mistakes borne out of nonchalance or narcissism. Anyone at the top of their game, whether in sport, business or whatever field, knows that there will always be people who want to be as good if not better than them and who will not assume too much in their quest to take your place.

Part Two
Confidence for life

Introduction

You've now enriched your knowledge about the different aspects of real life confidence and what it is and what it isn't. You've also begun to learn from some of the powerful and diverse real life stories from people in and out of the public eye and what part confidence has played in their lives and their setbacks and successes.

All this will already be changing the way you think and feel about your own confidence levels. And it will continue to give you a more realistically encouraging perspective and a greater sense of hope that you can acquire the confidence you need to achieve what you want to in life, no matter how small or significant.

This next part of this book will give you a great mix of ideas and strategies for applying it in a variety of everyday work and non-work scenarios – some of them colourfully random – so you can start building your confidence to make an immediate difference to your life and the lives of others.

Chapter 5

Confidence for work-life situations

We spend more time working and worrying about work than we do living in our non-work worlds – unless of course you're resolutely unemployed or a lady who lunches while steadfastly wearing Gucci.

For most of us, our job is the source of our income and therefore our lifestyle and, above all, our public and self-image. And this is where the problems with confidence can start as we feel we are what we do. This can make our work life seem restrictive and more pressured, because of the demands it makes of us and has to make of us, and therefore our confidence levels get pegged by pay, position and politics.

Although there is a lot of truth in this, work does not define us completely as people as there is more to us than our job or business area … unless of course you're an estate agent or a traffic warden. I've met all sorts of people in life, but have you actually met a traffic warden at a party – ever?! No. I thought not. They just don't get invited. Either that, or they pretend to be estate agents.

There are so many ways we can be pigeonholed in terms of our employment sphere, our job title, our income and even by what we tend to wear for work. Imagine if investment bankers wore blue and strategically soiled overalls and navvies wore smart trousers and tailored shirts and jackets. The world would have an image crisis and people would walk around feeling unnervingly confused and look at everyone else oddly, wondering if in fact a man in overalls, with a trilby hat tilted at a jaunty angle, was actually a tax inspector with the Inland Revenue or a lion tamer from Penge called Gervase.

The British in particular are very good at 'placing' people in their social context by what they 'do' professionally, how they 'do' it socially and who they 'do' in … ahem … more private parts of their lives. And we are all very aware of what others think, aren't we.

Many of us are so affected by what others think and feel about us, that when we sense them judging us we inadvertently and subconsciously allow them to dictate the way we live our lives and, above all, influence how we feel about ourselves. They affect our confidence when it is us, as individuals, who should decide how we feel about ourselves, not everyone else, no matter what our or their job or job title.

How you dictate your level of confidence

One key method for changing your approach is reverse visualisation. Imagine how you would feel if someone you met, professionally or socially, was unsure of who they were and how they came across, leaving you with the impression that they didn't think much of themselves. You would think of them in a negative light. Would you feel a keen need to socialise with them or even recommend or recruit them for a potential job? Probably not, because we need to be around people, both personally and professionally, who have a positive sense of self and purpose.

So how do you come across at work or socially? Do you give the right impression? It's your decision how you feel about yourself and what you project and that could be the difference between you connecting with someone for your (mutual) gain and they claiming a sudden need to get away from you, to leave the country and live under an assumed hairstyle.

A very, very accomplished person I know, in both their professional and personal lives, once told me that the person they respect most in the world, their father, was unemployed for great chunks of his life. It was because of how he has perceived himself, whatever his professional situation, and how he has treated others as a result. He was and still is a source of great strength, love and inspiration to his family and others and he comes across in this way as he has always determined to believe in himself, no matter how tough things have become. He made the decision early on to take control of how he feels about himself and has never allowed others to dictate, consciously or subconsciously, who he is as a person or as a working or even non-working man.

He has always been someone who people sense has something 'different' and 'special' about him. They have found themselves drawn to him because he has been as authentic as he has been quietly confident in himself which, in turn, has made him even more attractive to employers and highly regarded when, as a result, they have wanted to employ him.

Whether you're worried about your job, have lost it or even are doing well, remember circumstances change and so do other peoples' perceptions. They both vary like the wind – sometimes turbulent, sometimes calm. So it's for you to decide to be the rock that remains unaffected by whatever economic or employment elements you have to experience. You dictate your level of confidence – not other people.

So, if you're reading this after giving someone a parking ticket or even getting their vehicle towed away, please try to get yourself invited to a party – even if you have to claim to be an estate agent to do so – and declare yourself and your job proudly to the assembled company. That will test your confidence. You could be surprised. Mind you, you could also be asked to leave.

Several years ago I was at a snooty party in Notting Hill in West London when I claimed to be a traffic warden after meeting too many insincere people trying to place me in their societal pecking order. And I was even more surprised when I realised, despite my straight-faced flippancy, that they believed me! It showed how exuding confidence can improve peoples' perceptions … until I threatened to get one of the most affected guests (and there was some stiff competition on that score!) towed away.

The important thing is to STOP worrying about your apparent lack of confidence. Worrying about it gives it significance – a significance it doesn't deserve – and that will reinforce any unnecessary and unhelpful self-doubt.

Job interview

Character is more important than competence

In many cases, a potential employer will have made up their mind on whether you're right for the job before you even sit down to talk with them. The first thing people will judge you on is how you come across on a personal level. In short: whether you come across as a truly pleasant person. So your character is as important, if not more so, than your professional competence.

I have interviewed various people over the years. They all had varying approaches. One guy, good looking but with an air of tired intolerance, came for a job in a TV station I worked for. He wanted to walk straight into a job like mine as a presenter and a reporter despite having no proper qualifications apart from a large ego which showed great promise for rapid development. In some ways, ideal for TV! He sat there without a shred of humility and couldn't understand why we hadn't offered him a job on site. He left, disappointed, to become a lawyer.

When I was working for a dotcom back in the days when the investment money was produced almost before the business plan, a pulsatingly confident and attractive young woman came for an interview for an editorial position. She had shrewdly checked beforehand who was interviewing her, which explained her dress sense. I don't think I've ever seen such a low cut top in a work meeting, complete with a cleavage-squeezing push-up bra. Mind you, I've never worked in advertising. So who knows what's acceptable there.

She kept on wheeling herself closer to me in her chair as if she herself were on casters and then leaning over to give me the full benefit of her décolletage while looking at me with a subtle coquettishness. That would have been pleasantly enticing if we'd been in a social situation, like a bridge evening, as it's a card game that has never got me excited. But, even then, despite her flattering dirndl-like outfit, I didn't hire her for two reasons:

■ She was trying too hard to be a physically attractive employment prospect and was unnatural. She thought the more she purred and pulsated the more employable she would be. But I just didn't trust her.
■ She assumed that all she had to do was flash her pert breasts at me and speak with a steely sensuality and I'd roll over and beg her to sign on the dotted line, while dribbling with as much dignity as I could muster under the circumstances. Perhaps if *she* had rolled over then I might have been better disposed to her (irregular) humility.

There is a third way and it's the easiest. Be yourself. Be natural. It takes a lot less effort to have a greater impact, unlike the swaggerers, with their sense of self-entitlement, and the cleavage squeezers of this world who employ a lot more effort for much less potential return.

When to declare your weak points

In a study carried out in the 1970s at Duke University participants were asked to judge a man talking about his life and to rate the degree to which he sounded likeable.[9] Different groups of participants listened to different versions. Some heard the man reveal that he had missed a semester because he had been expelled for cheating. Those who heard this confession at the start thought he appeared far more likeable whereas the other half, who heard him declare this at the end, thought he didn't seem as likeable. The same study found that when the reason for missing the semester was due to something good like a prestigious scholarship, the reverse happened, because people thought he was being boastful.

This shows that, in an interview, the weak points should be declared at the beginning and the good points at the end. This has been confirmed by additional research that shows that lawyers are perceived to have a stronger case if they present weaknesses in their argument at the start of a trial. This shows confidence.

Listening and likeability

As likeability is so important, it would give a better impression if you:

- Ask questions of the interviewer(s) about their organisation and, if you can, about them. You can do this by listening to what they say about their non-work lives to pick up on where they live, their hobbies and interests and views.

- Talk about something about the organisation that you truly like and don't be afraid to compliment them.

- Be warmly enthusiastic about the job and the organisation, but not gushingly so.

■ Smile and maintain eye contact with your interviewers. And remember that as much as you have to impress them, they have to entice you.

Plan to prosper

To give a confident performance, you also have to take action and plan for the interview:

■ You have to work out what you have to offer them and why you're a great prospect on various fronts.

■ You also have to think about all the questions they could ask you, good, bad or bizarre, and also think of the questions you should ask them. This will give you confidence as will the fact that, as much as you have to appeal to them, they have to appeal to you.

■ If you put both them and yourself on the same level rather than putting them on a pedestal, you will come across as more confident and capable and therefore more employable.

REAL LIFE STORY

David Morrissey is an award-winning TV, film and stage actor and a TV director. He is considered to be one of the most versatile British actors of his generation. He has been in a wide range of films such as *Captain Corelli's Mandolin*, *The Other Boleyn Girl* and *Hilary and Jackie*, to name but a few. He won a Royal Television Society Best Actor Award for his portrayal of the ex-British Prime Minister Gordon Brown in *The Deal*.

'You need a certain level of confidence to meet life's challenges. You have to have a level of confidence and competence to take on certain types of work. But you don't want someone who's overconfident to the point of being arrogant. That's not an attractive quality.

'I grew up in a very loving and secure working-class background in Liverpool; but still, when I was younger, I wasn't terribly confident.

'As I've become more experienced as an actor I've become more confident in certain areas of my acting, but also the older I get the less confident I become in other areas. As an actor you tend to indulge your insecurities because that gives you a frisson. As an actor you want a certain level of unpredictability, you want some insecurity and nervousness. It's a very insecure profession anyway.

'So you're constantly playing with those levels of insecurity so, when you're performing, it's not dead; you're not just saying the line; there is some life in there.

'As an actor, you're always in competition. It's the whole nature of being an actor and the fact that you're being judged and appraised all the time. Those insecurities never go away. You expect them to go away as you get older and wiser, but they don't.'

David doesn't try to get too bothered about any unfavourable reviews of his work, 'unless there's some kernel of truth there'.

'I try to be my own critic about what I'm doing and I try to have people around me whose opinion I respect and who are honest – friends and family. And that's always a good thing for me. The other thing an actor has to do is take risks. You have to try things. You have to be open to new areas of work. You will get bad reviews, but that doesn't stop you being experimental and brave in your work. Trying to be safe all the time is a dead area.

'You've constantly got to be challenging yourself to do things differently. That's the type of actor I like to watch and see. I like to be around people who take risks. Sometimes those risks will come off and sometimes they won't.'

No matter how many disadvantages people feel they have that might stop them from acquiring confidence, David said that 'it's about being inside one's life, setting one's own challenges. I like to constantly remind myself of what I'm doing right at the moment rather than what I could have been doing when "this could have happened" or "that could have happened". I am capable of getting myself into a place like that, comparing myself to someone else or feeling I should be doing this or that.

'But rather, I look at my own life and think I'm very lucky here and living in quite a charmed place at the moment. And when I put things in perspective I have a certain amount of gratitude for the life I'm living. That's always a good thing rather than looking at another person and comparing. That has never led me to happiness.'

First day at a new office

Unfortunately, the first day at a new office is very much like the first day at a new, big school. But fortunately there are no double maths lessons and no detention. If there are, then don't accept the job!

Rather than feeling that everyone else already there knows the system better than you and finds it easier, you should instead tell yourself that you are bringing a new energy and new ideas that they may not have as well as a fresh and engaging way of working they may also not have. In effect, you need to think of yourself as a top professional footballer who's being transferred to another club that really wants you and your skills to help make them an even better and more successful outfit.

Office parties and work social get-togethers

The office party, certainly the Christmas one, is invariably a bubbling stew of banter, bonding, boozing or even bonking. Although such bacchanalian behaviour is not obligatory, some find the annual Christmas party a release from the months of work pressure and any smouldering sexual tension or simmering dislikes that may have been lurking beneath the reasonably ordered surface.

How to be natural in an unnatural environment

Although it's essential to have a laugh and enjoy yourself, there can sometimes be an awkward pressure to say the right thing to the right people or adopt a certain persona with your seniors, peers and juniors.

These supposedly relaxed social get-togethers are too often anything but that. Just because you're at the pub for a 'friendly drink' doesn't mean that it will be friendly. In fact, sometimes it's the complete opposite. It doesn't mean you can truly confide in your colleagues, tempting though that may be at times, certainly when you feel stressed and need an outlet for your pent-up emotions. Although this might be able to happen after you've got to know them over a long period of time.

I remember going for some so-called friendly drinks after work at one of the TV newsrooms I worked in. We all stood in a curved line – roughly in order of job title and self-importance – and pretended to chat normally. It was awful. It was tense, stilted and stiflingly political. Everyone was afraid of saying the wrong thing to the right person and the right thing to the wrong person. We kind of all knew that, as nights out go, this was almost as desperate as removing a toilet blockage with your bare hands – only the latter would have been more useful.

I remember talking in a relaxed and normal manner to some of the people around me, which perturbed them. They couldn't understand why I wanted to try and enjoy myself by having a normal conversation rather than paying superficial homage to the Editor or Senior Programme Producer. I only went once, despite several invitations, complete with the exhortation that 'it will be a laugh!' A laugh a decade, more like.

Hardly any of the people who endured that and other similar social torments were confident enough to be themselves. They tried too hard to be something they were not in the hope it would help others' perceptions of them and therefore their position within the company. The irony is that anyone who was confident enough to be themselves by just being natural would have created a better impression.

Having confidence also means not being afraid to leave before the others, if you have to, and certainly if you're being sucked into a grin and grovel fest. You may feel awkward as you leave, feeling that people may talk about you, even conspiratorially, after you have gone. Remember that they may actually admire you for having the confidence to leave – for whatever reason – and may even say something nice about you. But if they do say something unflattering – that I'm sure would be untrue – then it should not diminish who you really are or the talents you have.

Unless you are a complete and utter Muppet, professionally speaking, any unflattering remarks may well be made out of envy because those people do not have the personal and professional confidence or competence that you have. It's also a way of trying to shift the focus from their own insecurities and inadequacies. They don't live in a happy place, whereas you can. Just knowing that such people – and there are far too many of them out there – allow themselves to get chewed up to the extent that they want to bring other people down to their tormented level should give you the confidence to adopt a more positive view of yourself.

What you perceive about yourself is what you project about yourself, and what you project is what will colour other people's perceptions of you and therefore help reinforce how you perceive yourself, and so on and so forth.

Pitching to potential and existing clients

The importance of competence

In business, people tend to judge you on two things: character and competence. And the former invariably has more to do with how you get on than the latter. In a work environment, potential and existing clients tend to assume a certain and, one hopes, acceptable level of competence. That is unless you're the useless estate agent I kept on having foisted on me when I was looking for a home to buy several years ago.

Tom may have been a gangly and gormless twenty something, but he wasn't a bad person. It's just that he was completely incompetent and never seemed to try to do anything about it. He made one viewing appointment for the same property three times. On the first occasion he didn't turn up. On the second, he forgot the keys. And on the third the owner, who obviously felt the same as I did, refused to let him in and this was further reinforced by his disastrous attempts to try to persuade her otherwise. For instance, using the 'It's cloudy out here' line didn't sway her at all. This baffled him. The only reason I got in to see this property was because I persuaded the owner to let me in – if need be, without Tom. And then, when we finally got in, he proceeded to get all the details wrong, obviously quoting the specifications from another property in a different part of the city! A true Muppet.

Just seconds to impress

Alas, Tom was an awareness-free zone, which further blighted his character. So take hope – even if you're reading this book Tom which, in itself, would be encouraging – that even if you're not a star performer, a good character will get you a long way. People will have formed an opinion about you within three to five seconds of first seeing you. That impression can be set in stone in their minds within 30 seconds. This is known as the Primacy Effect which is the tendency for the first piece of information you are presented with to be more influential than those presented subsequently. So, even if you meet someone on numerous occasions after that first meeting, it will be mainly the picture or movie of that first encounter that your mind will refer to.

Getting into a tangle by trying too hard

People often struggle with how to behave with a potential client or an existing one. Respectfulness can turn unhelpfully into reverence and, at the other end of the behavioural scale, chumminess can turn into contract-ceasing cockiness. At a time when you most need to be yourself, it's very easy not to be. A potential client will often choose you, not just because they like your service and/or your products and the value they believe they will add to their business, but because they buy into you as a person.

Put yourself in their position. If someone was trying to do business with you, who would you prefer to deal with:

- The cocksure, super slick, hard-selling type who can somehow make you feel as if you want to appeal to or appease them?

- The politely awkward, slightly gauche, unconfident type for whom you want the presentational torment to finish, for their sake, and even yours as it makes you and them feel uneasy?

- The person with an air of warm authority about them, complemented by a warm smile and an understated respectfulness, who comes across as natural and engagingly enthusiastic and who is honest about the strengths and weaknesses of their product and/or service?

The person in option 3 is the most appealing to deal with. And that's how you should try to be. People want to do business with people they like and feel they can get along with. And by being yourself and believing in yourself you are more likely to come across more naturally and as a result inspire confidence in those you want to inspire confidence in.

How taking centre stage will help you win

Positioning yourself in the middle of a group of people in a meeting will increase your chances of making a good impression. Psychologists found that contestants in the TV programme 'The Weakest Link' who stood in the middle of the semi-circle reached the final round on average 42% of the time and won the game 45% of the time. But those standing at the more extreme positions reached the final round just 17% of the time and won just 10% of the time.[10] This is known as the Centre Stage effect.

I have been paid to speak in front of thousands of people over the years, from varying cultures and countries, ages and professional and personal backgrounds. And by the same token I have seen many other speakers perform, some wonderfully and some dreadfully.

The first thing to remember is that your audience responds to you and how you feel about yourself and your subject as you portray both at the same time. If you're nervous, it will make them uneasy. If you're relaxed, particularly when things go wrong, then they'll admire you even more for not being fazed by the situation. Rather than distracting their minds with your uneasiness and nerves and lack of confidence, they'll be able to focus on what you're saying. And that's the point of the event, surely.

Research has shown that persuading people in a large group is easier than persuading an individual as the more people there are in a group the more likely they are to comply with whatever the leader is saying. In group settings, people tend to be led by the unconscious minds of the rest of the group. And the average intelligence of the unconscious mind is that of a six year old!

Another tip is that when people are sitting there looking at you impassively, it's very easy for you to think that they're bored or don't like you. The thing is, you have been that person in the audience. Unless the speaker really is boring and/or unlikeable, you will have sat there thinking that they are not only very likeable but also very interesting; but you're not always going to express that facially. If somebody in my audience is sitting there with a maniacally animated and gleeful look on their face, they begin to worry me. I call security!

Difficult colleagues

Getting to know your colleagues' reality

Difficult colleagues come in various forms: they might be a boss, someone of the same rank or somebody junior. It's very easy to believe that they are behaving in this way because there is something about you that is wrong. But, in many cases, someone can be difficult because they are discontented about something in their work and/or home life. This makes them unhappy and so it adversely affects their attitude.

It could be because they have problems with their marriage or perhaps their partner isn't happy with them. It could be because your colleague may not be happy with themselves anyway. That will also have affected their emotional relationships. The problem is that if they let rip at home and have a go at their partner it would make matters a lot worse. So the next available outlet is work colleagues who, rightly or wrongly, may become more irritating to them as a result.

Therefore, trying to get to know your colleague will help you understand whether this might be the case. If so, that understanding about them should give you a constructive context and therefore some reassuring confidence that their fear or frustration is what's been getting to them rather than you.

Being honest with yourself

However, irrespective of any issues outside work, you could be a cause of irritation to them, justly or unjustly. So you have to ask yourself as objectively as you can whether there is something about your behaviour and your work that could have made them behave unhelpfully with you. This will give you a greater insight into the situation and yourself. It takes courage to do this, but it will make you stronger as a person.

If you're realistic with yourself, there will be times when you realise you could have done something better or not at all, as well as times when you know that you didn't do anything wrong. Being honest with yourself is not so scary; it can in fact be strangely reassuring. This is because you don't have to bear the subtle and sometimes gnawing pressure of living with the fact that there might be something about you or a situation that you could improve but haven't yet done so. That feeling will always be lurking there ready to weigh you down. So addressing such matters honestly will help you develop confidence by, acknowledging it, firstly, and, secondly, by then being able to deal with and improve things.

REAL LIFE STORY

Lisa had one major episode at work with a colleague in Human Resources who severely damaged her confidence.

'Through a misunderstanding, the head of HR called me into her office and accused me of treating employees poorly. She then proceeded to tell me that now she understood why people complained about me and why people didn't like me. I was young and it was my first real job so I didn't understand at the time how completely inappropriate it was. She said these things to me for about an hour, for most of which I was crying my eyes out. I left with a swollen face and red puffy eyes,' said Lisa.

'Some of my subordinates asked me what had happened. I wouldn't tell them at first, afraid of what she had said to me. After some time, I told a couple of them. They were incredulous. Not only had they not said anything about me, they hadn't even heard anything like that from others. I had cried myself to sleep for a month over what the head of HR said to me.

'It was at that point I decided one very important thing that led to a lot of changes: I am a good person and I deserve to be treated well. I always do what I think is the right thing. It was at that point that I started eliminating people from my life if they didn't treat me well. Anyone who made me feel bad about myself wasn't worth my time. I'm so much happier now. I've been following my dreams and am now an MBA student learning Chinese in Beijing and am currently working for a start-up as an intern,' she added.

Lecherous colleagues

The irony about lecherous people at work is that they have the confidence in the first place to think that they can come on to you in such a clumsy and crass way, thinking that you're bound to fall for their slavering form of seduction. Salacious and seedy chat, along with the odd fluid ounce of saliva ready to foam at the prospect of the delights they hope you hold in store for them, are off-putting. If such approaches do work on you, then your confidence levels must be low! But hopefully not.

How to turn the tables

Such behaviour can get worse, certainly over time. But how you deal with it is crucial. A quietly confident approach is the best way of pricking their bubble and will help cut their behaviour short there and then. This involves two principal approaches:

Be pleasantly firm and calm, telling them that they're being inappropriate / unfunny / unattractive / instantly reportable / subsequently sackable (choose accordingly) and that it's not the way to win your heart or friendship – or anyone's, for that matter. You can add that you should both leave it there, say and do no more. End of story.

Play them at their own game, saying that you just love their (fatuous) flirtations and the way they make those (crass) remarks and their (revolting) physical gestures. If that doesn't dampen their tacky ardour then why not embarrass them by inviting some of your (same sex) colleagues over and asking the letch to try some of their lines and manoeuvres on them too. Do it with a big smile and a sense of high energy fun. The smiling mockery will not only make others aware of the lecherous colleague's behaviour, it should humble them enough to stop. Now, taking the latter approach may make them want to leave the country and live under an assumed facial expression; but, needs must.

Banter and flirtation

There is another level of confidence that comes into play in dealings between members of the opposite sex in a work environment. Banter and even good-hearted flirtation are part of many workplaces. But this doesn't include many government departments where no one knows how to flirt because they haven't developed a training course for it yet or because it's been ruled out on Health & Safety grounds, like so many things have been.

People have become too precious about interactions with members of the opposite sex that would normally be deemed natural interactions, certainly outside work. It's one thing for a woman to complain that a man pinched her bum or groped her breasts or flashed what he could at her from the unfastened zip of his trousers, and that is unacceptable, but quite another for her to claim tens or even hundreds of thousands of pounds worth of legal damages due to the 'trauma' of having some well meaning man flattering her for having a great suit or teasing her back in a bout of banter.

Women sexually harassing men

Women, who are a rapidly growing force in the working world, also tease and flirt with men and, as I know from personal experience, are just as capable of sexually harassing a man as men are with women. The problem with the former is that people jokingly think a man will love being sexually harassed because men are always meant to be 'up for it'. I doubt many men would want to be 'up for it' with a woman who, despite her quite senior position within a company, was humourless, bitter and whose body odour tended to kick in the closer we got to the end of the day, just before we went on air.

Admittedly, the constant phone calls late into the night at my home urging us to get together at her place so she could 'help' me out within the company, and the way she rubbed her sizeable breasts against me as I was sitting down in a quiet edit suite working to desperate deadlines, didn't really help her create a very good impression in my mind of a normal and warmly appealing woman who was sane. And I had never given any sign of interest in her at all.

This sort of experience can affect your confidence. As much as it's flattering to be desired, it's not comforting to be hounded by a horny harridan. You can't relax for fear of how they're going to react and what they're going to do to you next, directly or behind your back. And as you can't be completely yourself, it can undermine the way you regard yourself.

But you have to remind yourself that there's nothing wrong with you and that you must see the process through and stand your ground, otherwise something will happen which will seriously dent your confidence.

That happened to me when she tried to get me fired for doing something I hadn't done after she found out I had started dating someone else. I made sure a few well placed people with integrity knew what had been happening and told myself I wasn't going to change to comply with her warped wishes or be just as aggressive back when she tried to get me fired. This strategy worked as nothing came of her attempt to have me booted out for, in effect, not reciprocating her emotional and sexual urges and, even worse in her mind, then dating someone other than her. But it certainly made me more inhibited and cautious.

On occasions like this, having genuinely good support from close colleagues and a trustworthy manager can help you with both your perspective and your sense of self which in turn will help maintain your confidence. If anything, it's easier for women in this position because people find sexual harassment by a woman towards a man less comprehensible.

There is a postscript to this story. Years later, I heard though a mutual acquaintance that this woman had had a breakdown, a result of years of unhappiness, some of it self-inflicted. That's why there was so much simmering anger and frustration in her, which sadly she inflicted on others.

Redundancy

Redundancy can appear to stop the safe and structured course of your life in its tracks. And if you aren't being made 'redundant', then perhaps you're experiencing the reality of transparent euphemisms like 'being retrenched' or 'letting you go'. The latter is plainly silly as it suggests you made the decision that you wanted to go so that you then struggle to pay your bills and feel useless for not having a job to go to.

You can be made redundant on the last in, first out approach. This is a short-sighted management practice because it ignores the fact that you might well be giving huge amounts of value to your employer and quite possibly even more than those who've been at the company longer. You can be made redundant because it's a numbers game and the company simply cannot afford to pay for someone with your remit or to pay for your unit or even office or factory. This ostensibly more impersonal approach can salve a bruised ego. But, how do you deal with it if it's personal?

How to cope when it's personal

I was once made redundant by a line manager who really disliked me and another colleague. It was purely personal. This is despite the fact that, being so ridiculously young in the job I was doing, I was paid less than any of my fellow TV news correspondents. And the much older fellow correspondent was an award-winning journalist.

Our line manager was a decidedly unpleasant individual. This man was unhappy, bitter and insecure and tried his hardest to make my life hell for a year. The whole process was draining and confidence sapping. But he was so vindictive for so long, that it got to the point that he became ridiculous, on all fronts. And this helped remind me that, even if I was not always perfect in my job and even if our personalities were different, that I wasn't so bad that I deserved this sort of vitriolic victimisation. I made sure I got the backing and support of other senior people as a counterbalance.

To help in this process, I also reminded myself that he was a bully – and bullies never win in the end. Invariably, the bully becomes one to mask his or her own fear that *they* might be bullied because they are afraid of not being good enough in some aspect of their personal and/or professional lives. So they try and pick on people who might expose these insecurities and inadequacies, either directly or indirectly, or those who they believe can't or won't fight back.

Also, if someone is good at their job, these types of people should be grateful for that and not try to crush up-and-coming people in their organisation. But, as is the way in life, there will always be some unpleasant and unhelpful people amidst the lots of great people you get to work and spend time with.

Another good way of dealing with a situation like this is to remind yourself of all your colleagues and others outside work who think you're great and rate you. Try to see why someone, like the spindly and spiteful cove I had to deal with, behaves like this:

- Are they unhappy in their work?

- Are they under huge pressure from their boss? Is that boss treating them in the way that they are treating you?

- Have you done or are you doing better than they were/are?

- Are you more popular than they are?

- Have you done something professionally or personally that upset them or let down your colleagues or even the company? How did others react to you after this?

- Is there something outside work that's affecting their behaviour? Do they have problems in their relationship or marriage or, as was invariably the case in TV news, both? Perhaps they are not in a relationship and are lonely and emotionally and/or sexually frustrated? Do they have few or no friends outside work? Do they not get invited out much, if at all?

- Is there anything else about you that could make them like this? Perhaps you are younger or they think you're more physically attractive, funnier or have better clothes?

- If you were them, with their issues and pressures, and faced with you, how would you act – really?

Once you've honestly thought about these questions, then learn from the answers. See it as an opportunity to become wiser and more able to deal with such situations in the future, or even how to avoid them. See it also as a great opportunity to seek new professional and even personal challenges.

Banishing the burden for a new beginning

When I was made redundant (the redundancy money helped), I remember feeling and then saying to those colleagues who were shocked, saddened and even outraged that I had been binned, that I had been wanting to go for a wee while and that the only difference was that I was given a (financial) helping hand!

I remember feeling that a huge and highly stressful and emotionally draining weight had been lifted off my much put-upon shoulders. Even though the British economy was sliding, with arms flailing desperately, into a muddy economic pit, I felt like I had my life back and that I could now achieve new and more exciting things. The trick is not to see it as the end, but as an exciting new beginning to something better in which you'll be wiser.

REAL LIFE STORY

Doug Richard is a UK-based Californian entrepreneur. He came to prominence as a result of the BBC TV programme 'Dragons' Den', where he appeared as a 'dragon' or investor in the first two series. He founded and sold two companies and between 1996 and 2000 was President and CEO of a US publicly quoted software company. In 2008 he founded the School for Startups, an enterprise focused on teaching entrepreneurship across the UK.

'In the world in which I work, namely starting a business, unfortunately confidence is almost everything in many ways. The question isn't whether you are confident but, how you act, whether you feel confident or not.

'So, imagine you're standing in the wings of a stage and in five minutes you have to go on and pitch in front of an audience of 1,000 people and the future of your entrepreneurial opportunity depends largely on how well you pitch. You're as nervous as hell, but in spite of how you feel and despite the fear, you put a smile on your face, take a deep breath and walk slowly to the centre of the stage, steel yourself, look them all in the eye and without hesitation or pause, calmly and with enthusiasm and passion, explain your position for the world. That is what you've got to be able to do. You need to be able to overcome your fear and do it anyway.

'I was always confident and I certainly didn't have any basis for my confidence. I used to joke that I was much more confident than I was competent. It was a lack of rigour at looking at risk, unfortunately, that led to my early confidence. I think I was optimistic more than I was confident. I know I suffered a lot of bumps along the road because of my blind optimism and I think, in some cases, it's better to be more thoughtful than merely confident.

'I do think it's more about courage than anything else. A lot of people are paralysed by fear and how other people will look at them when they fail. They see what can go right and they can see what can go wrong and they are aware of the downside and they can imagine it quite thoroughly whereas some people, like myself, spend time daydreaming about the upside and don't really pay much attention to the downside.

'You don't have to look very far to see examples of the most ordinary people achieving the most extraordinary things. If somebody says to me that I am not smart enough, not pretty enough, not fit enough, that I don't have the experience, or the education, or the resources or the background or the training, I say this: It's all possibly true. But for every time someone says one of those things to me I can remember someone else who didn't have that who then went on to succeed.

'We all have huge things that hold us back. I get very annoyed when a successful entrepreneur stands up and tells their life story and does so without the blemishes, without admitting that they didn't really know what they were doing or that they made mistakes, or admitting there were times when everything came perilously close to failure. In not admitting these things they make it seem, for others who haven't yet gone down that path, that it is in fact reserved for very few people who always get it right.

'The truth is that everybody mucks it up along the way. Everyone who is successful has a lingering doubt inside them as to whether they deserve it or not.'

When Doug walked away after selling his second company, his first software company, to a large US public software operation, he thought he was rich. He was in his thirties and he was given shares in return for his company. Doug had to hold onto the shares for 100 days before selling them to get his cash – a very common transaction.

He moved his young family to a large house in Texas to merge the two companies and got a big mortgage. But, on day 89, the shares in the parent company fell by 99% and he was wiped out. Millions of dollars of his had disappeared as had millions from his family and friends and other investors. There was chaos as the company was in financial freefall and no one was telling him what was going on. He 'had been screwed'.

'I was broke, without money, and in a bad mood!'

He became angry and wanted revenge. Then he became very brave.

'When you've lost everything, it costs very little to be brave, I've found.'

He challenged the management team and board and ended up doing a reverse takeover, taking over as CEO of the global US software company.

'It took four years of running that company to get my money back. And I was thoroughly unqualified. I'm still unqualified.'

After that episode he says he has never been afraid of anything. He now also does public speaking without notes or rehearsal.

Asking for a pay rise or promotion

Take action – every time

If you're going to ask for a promotion, more pay or even both, then you actually need to do it – not just talk about it, think about it or whinge about it. You need to take action. That's obvious, surely? Alas, no. As in life, many people talk about doing things, but very few actually do what they say they want to.

You must not feel guilty about asking. You have to believe you are worth it and that it makes sense for your organisation to make this happen for you before you even think of approaching your boss. But ask yourself: if you were your boss, why would you want to do this and how would it benefit the company? How do you give enough value to merit your financial and/or positional advancement?

Timing and location are crucial

Once you've prepared your case and, just as importantly, have worked out how to defend a case against you, then think about when and how you will ask your boss or whoever is the right person to speak with. The environment in which you ask someone for something is crucial. If, say, your male boss has just come out of the shower in the workplace changing rooms and you sidle up to him with a faux nonchalance and ask if he can give you a better package, then this will make him feel awkward – certainly if you're a woman. If you're a man doing the sidling, then the same applies. And I strongly suspect that even a throwaway compliment to try to effect a relaxed atmosphere – something like 'Nice buns. Do you work out?' – will not help him feel more relaxed about the situation. (In this case, leave the area immediately and claim you were doing a Tourette's syndrome role play.)

Chatting with them when they're fresh and not frantic, stressed or homicidal will help your cause. Ask them when there is a good time for a quick and private chat. It might be straight away or later on. Whatever time is chosen, then be pleased you've actually taken the active step of making the initial enquiry. So many duck out for fear of potential refusal and rejection and that can and will gnaw away at your confidence. It also doesn't earn you more pay or a promotion.

Homework, humility and humour

Feeling nervous beneath the surface is not a bad thing. In fact, it's healthy as the increase in adrenaline can be used to make sure you act in the most effective manner, coming across in a casually clever way. And even when you act with a warm calmness you will probably be pedalling frantically underneath. That is natural. Along with conveying a convincing surface impression, you also have to believe yourself fundamentally worthy of what you want because that is the vibe you will give off.

If you've done your homework and you truly believe you deserve it – without any expectation or sense of self-entitlement – then you will stand a much better chance of getting what you want. You need to approach your chat with ready supplies of humility and, if required, humour and a sense of polite and positive purpose. You also need to come across as if you not only like and admire the person you're asking but are enjoying your chat with them, whatever the outcome, because you genuinely believe in your cause and their desire to further that cause.

Now, if you don't like or admire them – alarmingly common – then try to find something about them that can help you to at least pretend to feel that way. Most people have some redeeming features. This is not about being obsequious, but about how they perceive you in the moment, as what you feel about them will be projected to their subconscious mind. And if you're thinking 'you're a snivelling little snerge', then, despite your best superficial efforts, which are likely to come across as superficial, they will feel that you think they are indeed a 'snivelling little snerge'. Neither the pay rise nor the promotion are likely to be forthcoming.

But if the two of you don't hit it off at all, then just play it straight and act with the same quiet but focused dignity. To pretend that someone with whom you share a mutual dislike is suddenly a really great and nice person will make you feel uneasy and come across as incongruent. And this will adversely affect your application. You must be resilient enough to realise that, in this tricky scenario, you might come away with nothing. They might dismiss you out of hand, even rudely.

If your application is rejected, then the resilient part of you will remind you that this does not mean that you're not worth it. You have to believe it. Accept that, despite the worthiness of your case, you will not always get what you want. Then you need a plan and perhaps patience to work out when you can have another go and through alternative channels, by which point circumstances might well have changed for the better.

Networking

The delicate art of true networking

Networking is a gentle yet powerful art. The right approach, which is in fact an easy one to acquire, will not only be very useful for your professional interests, opportunities and relationships, but it will also help develop your confidence which will, in turn, make you a better networker.

I earned more than £50,000 worth of business from attending just one event because of the people I met with whom I networked and developed a great working relationship.

Now, networking – true networking – is not about turning up and acting like the dealer in a sort of business card blackjack where you hand out your cards at regular intervals in the hope of immediate professional opportunity and financial return. It's about getting to know people, with whom you have developed some rapport, without expectation on either side, following up and then building and sustaining a relationship.

It's better to come away with two or three business cards from people with whom you had a great chat and connection, than swagger off at the end of the meeting with a pocketful of cards from people you can barely remember and who probably feel the same about you.

How to get someone to like you

So understanding this hopefully makes you feel under less pressure, which should in turn make you feel more confident, as should the fact that most other people at these events feel the same way. Remember that the kind of people others are drawn to and want to chat with are those who appear most at ease with themselves, who are warm and welcoming and who put you at your ease and make you feel as if they're really pleased to meet you.

The father of the multi-millionaire pop mogul Simon Cowell is said to have told him that whenever he met someone he should imagine above their head, writ large in bright neon letters, the words 'MAKE ME FEEL IMPORTANT'. It doesn't take much confidence to make someone feel like this; but the way you make them feel and the way they can then react to you will make you feel as great as they do. And that will further strengthen your confidence.

On the other hand, if you're nervous or awkward then you can come across as defensive and others are less likely to come and talk to you. This is because, firstly, others will feel ill at ease with you because you look like a Trappist monk who's suddenly found himself most inconveniently at a drinks party. Secondly, you will be transmitting a 'this conversation will be hard-going, so enter my space at your peril' look. It's not about being a wise-cracking extrovert, but about being at ease with yourself, quietly or otherwise.

Remind yourself of at least three great things about you and three things, whether information, contacts or experiences, that could be of interest or of use to those you chat with. Giving to people will make you stand out from all those who want to get something from other people just for themselves. And there are lots who are 'on the make'.

Enter a room with dignified enthusiasm and smile. That is when people are most likely to notice you and whether you're worth talking to. You may be feeling awkward and even nervous, certainly if you don't know anyone, but take action by making a determined effort to walk with as much presence as you can muster. Nothing Shakespearian. Just walk tall, smile and pause. Never look rushed as if you desperately need to dive for social cover, stage left or right. Remember that even though people are likely to be huddled together in groups, most of them couldn't walk into a room with eye-catching aplomb and will probably have anchored themselves to a group of people they haven't got the confidence to escape from when they need to.

So see yourself as the answer to all their social occasion ills. Go over to someone you like the look of and say hello, smile and get to know them and put them at their ease. They will be grateful for it and this will help bring the best out of them. It will also make you feel less nervous and help you to realise a new found level of confidence. Talking is such a natural thing and yet, in these situations, people seem to find it difficult. It's as if they've suddenly been asked to give the State of the Union speech without any preparation or without even knowing anything about the USA. People conjure up unhelpful social fears in their minds, so your trick is to help them realise that talking to a warm and interested human being like you is actually reassuringly enjoyable.

There's also another factor here. People always hope someone else will make the effort to initiate a conversation and then sustain it so they can just add to it when they feel they've got something to say. Too many people are fundamentally lazy in these networking situations. They will talk to people they know, ideally ones they like, but will hope someone like you will come along and add some snap, crackle and pop to the situation. It doesn't take much: a warm smile while saying hello, accompanied by a proper handshake and you asking for their names and then addressing every person in the group as if you're looking forward to actually getting to know them. By doing this, you will come across as confident and that will in turn make you feel more confident because of the way people will react to you. And you will find these scenarios more manageable and so you will therefore get more out of them.

The difference between confidence and arrogance

A word of caution, though. Some people come across with a loud 'drink me in, you lucky people' swagger. That's not confidence. That's theatrical arrogance or people trying too hard to appear confident. And that's off-putting for those in their audience. I say 'audience' because that's how such people can see those they prance about in front of. Now, if you're on a roll and are being genuinely entertaining and energising, that's great. It's being forcefully fake that jars with people because, if you're on the receiving end of this, you will feel the swaggerer is only interested in you being interested in them.

Dating work colleagues

In most full-time jobs we tend to spend more time – certainly quality time – with our work colleagues than our loved ones, whether partners, family or friends. Therefore it's not surprising that we get to know our colleagues very well. We see them, and they us, at their very best and at their very worst. Because of the demands and sometimes delights of work we tend to be at our best during working hours and, certainly, during the tougher times, need a receptive human connection to help us deal with the stress and strains of our jobs.

So, if you like the cut of somebody's jib, you have an advantage because the chances are you will both have had numerous opportunities to get to know each other – and that gives you a head start. A lot of the banter, nay flirting, has already been taking place, if you get on really well, so this makes it a lot easier to ask someone out as, in effect, you've already been dating. The main thing is to take action. Just do it.

This is fine if you're single. But if you or the object of your desire is already in a relationship, then this will have implications that cannot just erode your confidence, but shatter the confidence of the people who would have been cheated on.

I remember one of my TV news colleagues using the 'And Finally…' slot at the end of one news broadcast to tell the man she wanted that she loved him and wanted to live 'in passion' with him. It went out live. We were all gobsmacked. Mind you, not as much as another man who was meant to be her boyfriend and the woman who we all thought was the partner of the man she declared herself to. I remember this inspiring a spate of such cringeworthy declarations live on air – all just as gauche and awkward.

One woman, a weather forecaster as I recall, did exactly the same to the programme producer as he sat in the gallery during a live programme. I'll never forget his look of shock, embarrassment and reasonably suppressed irritation that this had occurred. After he started to regain his composure, I seem to recall him telling her that declaring her love and proposing to him on air was not the best place to do it.

So, as much as confidence can give you the impetus to do something daring and different, to do what many others would be afraid to do, you should believe in yourself enough not to do something that makes people squirm, certainly live on air.

Getting dumped by a colleague after an intimate encounter

It doesn't matter how you try to dress this one up – this is tricky, certainly if you were dumped because you had some noisy and unappealing habit or because you became too clingy or an emotional and sexual Caligula. You may have been none of these. It may have been that you were just not suited, despite months or even just minutes of workplace chemistry that, as it turned out, once you'd thrown caution, spreadsheets and Y-fronts to the wind, was only going to survive one short intimate outburst.

Never lose your dignity, no matter how the person behaves afterwards. You may have spent a night of wild indifference in each other's arms or even have been trussed up together like a pair of Christmas turkeys, while yelping in a Welsh accent, to get your sexual thrill. But somehow this may not have worked for one or both of you on a personal level. At the time, it seemed liked an excellent way to celebrate your lust, but then reality kicked in and now you're both very embarrassed by it all.

This embarrassment may be compounded by the fact that the other person, or even you, has confided in a trustworthy colleague who, so burdened by this bizarre revelation, has had to share it, in confidence, of course, with some other trustworthy soul who, in turn, struggles to deal with it on their own. And so on and so forth.

You will need resilience, acceptance and belief to help you get the confidence to deal with this so that it doesn't affect you personally as well as professionally. On a positive note, you will be the first person your Christmas office party organisers turn to, come the yuletide party season, to see if you can do a special turn. But you may decide you have to decline this rib-tickling request. This could be because of your own performance modesty or because you feel your trussed-up Christmas turkey routine, complete with Welsh gurgling, needs freshening up and isn't quite ready for a wider public.

If you feel you can't take confidence from this appreciation of your unusual talent, then try to imagine how you would regard the subject of such a revelation at work. If they're awkward and shrink into their shell, then you will think less of them. They will sense this and their confidence will be undermined. But if, after Turkeygate or Gobblegate, the protagonist accepts that he or she has been … a bit … ahem … unusual, but still believes in themselves and is resilient enough to know that it won't affect the way they do their job, then others are more likely to admire them for having the courage to face up to the colourful indignity and indelicacy of what's happened.

Dealing with alpha males

How women can deal with an alpha male

My wise grandmother once said: 'Never make a woman feel plain and never make a man look stupid.' Just as women want to feel attractive and desired, men want to be admired. And that's all down to male pride. Male pride, for most men, is a potent mixture of testosterone and ego, mixed with a need for achievement and admiration, to prove a man is worthy of being desired by women and admired also by his male peers. It takes confidence and good communication to deal with an alpha male, certainly one in full strut!

1. No woman should try to out-alpha an alpha male. That won't work because alpha males like women, whether or not they're alpha females, to act like women and not like men. To see it from a woman's perspective: how would you, as a woman, feel if an alpha male you know started to behave in a more feminine way, trying to be one of the girls? Not only would it be ineffective for the man, but he would then immediately have his alpha licence revoked and be made by his mates to wear mismatched bra and panties in his local gym and/or his local pub.

2. If you want to try and subdue and conquer an alpha male, expect a fight, and an ugly one, at that! Allow the man the time to flex whatever the man has to flex to assert his credentials, unless he is doing so in a plainly offensive way. In that case, don't be afraid to challenge him with a cool, collected charm if there's something he's said or done which you disagree with or aren't sure about.

3. An alpha male will want a woman to be impressed by him in some way, even more so if he feels the woman is worth impressing. To the alpha male, most women are a legitimate target in this regard because they've been hard-wired that way since the days when they had to wrestle the odd diplodocus to the ground to get the attention of a cave woman who took their fancy and who also handily rustled up a fine Stone Age dinosaur dish.

4. As much as some alpha males like the idea of a woman being wowed by them unquestioningly, the reality is that such a woman will soon prove increasingly less challenging and any such admiration or ardour will soon lose its impact on the man.

5. Alpha males like to challenge themselves and overcome obstacles and win. So they are prepared to get stuck in to a good bout of psychological, practical and even physical fisticuffs to achieve what they're aiming for. Now, although most men have a pretty good idea of how other men will operate in this gladiatorial arena, there will be many who feel they don't know how a female opponent will behave. And this can unsettle them and

therefore work to your advantage. So be prepared for a pre-emptive strike... on both sides!

6. Use your humour, your feminine charm, your intelligence, your passion and stand your ground. If done like this, most men will find it hard to resist someone who they believe allows them to be an alpha male, but, at the same time, wants to be heard as much as the man, and has 'the balls', as it were, to stand up for themselves.

7. Respect is important. As much as an alpha male wants to be respected, he wants to deal with a woman he can respect. For the woman, this will take courage and resilience – being able to take the banter and the peacock feather waving – as well as the self-belief to feel you can hold your own.

8. Just as women want men to understand them, no matter how complicated or contrary some women may be, men also want to be understood by women, no matter how complicated or challenging some men may be. So women should ask their opinions on certain work and other issues. Get them to talk. It will flatter their ego and make them feel you value them enough to ask for their thoughts and feelings. In that scenario, unless they feel it is a conversational trap, most men are happy to expound.

9. Be prepared to talk a man's language – and not be offended by it – as well as talk a woman's language in a way men can engage with.

10. Don't expect special treatment just because you're a woman. That is guaranteed to irritate most if not all men. It will work against you, even more so if you take internal and/or external proceedings because you took exception, say, to a colourful piece of male banter or even a genuine compliment about your appearance. Just because a man remarks how well or stylish you look does not necessarily mean he rates you less professionally or personally or wants to do things with you that will raise more than one eyebrow and steam up your office windows.

How men can deal with an alpha male

Men are naturally competitive with other men, certainly if an alpha male perceives a threat from another alpha male. Beta males can either get ignored or bulldozed by the more combative, assertive and even arrogant alpha. And, if women are present, the alpha male will be even more determined to impress them and come out on top. It's the way alphas are hard wired. It stems from the days when Cave Woman wanted to know that her hairy, grunting Cave Man could knock nine bells out of a diplodocus and drag it back home in time for dinner. So how can men deal with alpha males:

1. A lot of alphas will talk first and may listen later. The clever man, whether an alpha or beta, listens to the alpha expound, revealing his thoughts and ego levels. You learn and achieve more by listening first and talking second. This will help you tailor your approach to the alpha.

2. Stand your ground. An alpha will not respect any man who crumbles at the slightest stern facial expression, raised voice, jabbing finger or strutting stomp. Now standing your ground does not necessarily mean adopting stern facial expressions, raising your voice, jabbing your finger and stomping about like you own the joint. It's about keeping unblinkingly cool and calm and physically standing your ground so the message you send out is that you're not perturbed by any unsettling and intimidating behaviour. And this will help take the steam out of his bluff and bluster. And, particularly if an alpha is overdoing the Big I Am bit, he will start to look and feel increasingly silly. This will undermine him.

3. Don't be keen to please him in the hope he will not give you a hard time. If you do, you're a lost cause in the alpha's mind as he will

regard you as a beta, if not a gamma male. When dealing with the alpha your own self-respect and confidence will diminish as his increases.

4. Let alphas earn your friendship and respect – not the other way around. Alphas see themselves at the top of the personality pile and will often assume that people will respect and want to befriend them. If you do this unquestioningly, because you want a quiet life, then they will never respect you. But if you're friendly and make them feel that you'll give them time and listen, but on your terms, so you don't accept everything they say and do, then they're more likely to take you seriously.

5. Adopt the right body language. Stand up straight, walk tall, shake hands firmly, look them in the eye, smile with confident purpose and own the physical space in which you find yourself, as if no one could barge you out the way.

Breaking bad news to a colleague

Despite having the position and the power, too many people in management still struggle with telling someone that they're not getting a pay rise, that they are getting demoted, fired, punished or need to get a better haircut, clothes or even a life.

Avoiding the situation by not saying anything at all or getting someone else to say something will make matters worse, particularly for the person who needs to be communicated with. See it as a conversation. Ask yourself how you would like to be treated in this scenario. So prepare what you're going to say and also what they could say or even do to you in return. Get to the point and speak with a warm authority. Using visualisation, imagine yourself both during and certainly after the chat. Imagine your colleague accepting what you have said, even if you both found it hard, but with them appreciating the way you have dealt with the situation.

It's highly unlikely they're going to staple you to your desk or some such. It will be over and you both will have survived. For them, it will be a setback or an affront, depending on what the chat is about, but you will have shown courage in tackling something in the best way for them and you. The alternative – avoiding the situation – will just make the problem fester and your confidence levels recede because you didn't attempt something you not only had to do, but were capable of doing.

Your job image

There was a time when I went to a series of parties with other young professionals where I met too many accountants who sheepishly admitted their occupation. They kept on apologising for being accountants because of the job's dull, if not functional, public image. And some of them were even profuse in their professional and therefore personal self-denunciation. Now, some accountants have good reason to feel this way, but are too unexciting to admit this in case it makes them sound funny or intriguing. But there are many who aren't dull and who have good reason to feel proud of their professional status.

My father is a chartered accountant and businessman and he is one of the best men I know. In fact, he was the Best Man at my wedding. He's anything but boring and is an example of how a person should conduct their life.

When I met these apologetic accountants I told them I was crying out for one to declare, without irony, that they were proud to be an accountant and that they led a rewarding, stimulating and totally worthwhile existence. If someone did, wouldn't you prefer to do business with them rather than the self-confessed lobotomised bean counter?

And yet the same defeatist declarations were also uttered by people from the seemingly glamorous world of PR. As I also found out, if I told someone I was a national newspaper journalist or a network TV news correspondent – the very people whose editorial endeavours PR people try to steer in favour of their clients – then a lot of young PR people started getting twitchy. This is because they thought that proper journalists looked down on PR, as it can be the option for those who can't hack it in proper journalism. Again, more apologies for what they did.

The irony is that a lot of journalists look at the world of PR and think it's a much more civilised way of earning a living as it is better paid, with nicer hours and nicer people, on the whole. A further irony, but a healthier one, is that I've met plumbers and others who do what are often perceived as menial jobs who love what they do because it fulfils them on so many levels. In fact, they are the sort of people you want to work with.

Being genuinely enthusiastic

Expressing a genuine enthusiasm for your job, through your words and actions, shines a positive light on what is often a dimly lit undercurrent for many people: an unenthusiastic and uninspiring feeling about what they do for a living. Even though your positive view of your job might reinforce someone else's negative view of theirs, there will be a part of them that admires you and will be drawn to you. They will aspire to do something that makes them feel about their career as you do about yours. Whether or not they do something about it is not for you to worry about.

The point is that the many people with an uninspiring attitude to their work will rate you more highly because of your positive attitude. That will help boost your self-belief and confidence, even more so if, as a result of meeting you, someone wants to put work your way or recommend you to others, which will further strengthen your confidence. Is that likely to happen to the negative person? No way! And yet, how many people do you meet socially and professionally who are unenthused about their work life and are therefore uninspiring. There are far too many.

Changing your work life

So, take the opportunity to stand out by being a part of the inspiring minority. But only if you really do enjoy what you do. If you don't, then avoid talking negatively about it because you never know who might be listening to you and what opportunities there are. Do something about changing your work life for the better. I speak from experience.

When I was a freelance network TV news and radio correspondent it got to the point, in the end, where I simply hated my working life. I just fell out of love with what I was doing. It was a mixture of things: the odd hours, the lack of decent pay, the stress, too many negative and toxic egos, the bitter office politics and the fact that, despite being an award-winning journalist and broadcaster, I wasn't feeling valued at all. I had lost my sense of purpose and felt miserable.

This was made harder by the fact that because people I knew used to watch and hear me on the air, they assumed I had a wonderfully glamorous life of fame, fortune, fast cars, faster women and fancy parties with famous people. They would never have countenanced the fact that I actually didn't like the professional life I had any more. When people came up to me at parties and told me they had seen or heard me on the BBC, they were excited for me. But I wasn't. They thought I was being modest when I downplayed what I did. That wasn't the case. I just didn't want to talk about something that wasn't making me happy.

The irony about my job was that it wasn't so much the glamour, but the perception of glamour that fooled people. The picture people had of the working environment I was a part of was so at odds with the general reality. Some of my colleagues, whether 'on air' types or not, were some of the most broodingly unhappy and tense individuals even though they were at the zenith of the profession. The working environment and pressures didn't help, but even so.

They would complain that they weren't getting on air enough, that they didn't like the way another correspondent had done this or that piece to camera, they didn't like the hours, the pay or the conditions. They also complained they were having problems with their marriages. But then I pointed out that perhaps they shouldn't be shagging those other people who were, as a result, also having marital problems.

I found myself giving off the cuff mini motivational talks to them that I really enjoyed and that made them stop to think about what they were doing with their lives. It was something that was brought out when I went to a top career psychology organisation in London to help me find a new vocation. That day changed my life and led me to become an entrepreneur who helps people with their confidence and communication. I just love it and, even if I'm having a bad day, I always talk about what I do with passion and belief. And that's how I got my first client.

I was at a networking event, which I hadn't wanted to go to. I was very tired and going down with a bad cold and felt out of sync with everyone else there who was buzzing around frantically and, in some cases, naturally. I got talking to a charming girl who seemed to feel as I did. And when, one and a half minutes later, the conversation ran out, I suggested we talk to the main speaker who had given a short keynote speech. He was – and still is – a straight-talking alpha male.

When he asked her what she did, she mumbled something unsurely. With a look of rapidly receding patience, he asked her again. She mumbled a bit more before I answered for her by saying she was in consumer PR. He immediately turned around to me in the hope of getting a more engaging response. Even though I didn't feel like it, I smiled and told him what I did, adding various bits of colour to my description.

Within 45 seconds he had suggested we should work together. He later told me, when his company became my first client, that out of all the 60 or so people there, many of whom wanted to get work from him, I was the only person he even bothered meeting up with. He liked my confidence and belief in what I was doing and the enthusiasm and colour with which I spoke about it.

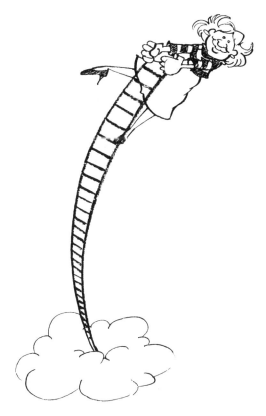

Starting your own business

Creating and then nurturing your own enterprise is one of the most challenging things you will ever do in your life. The risks are ten times greater, but then so are the rewards. However the great thing is that you create an opportunity to shape your life and also to make it more rewardingly adventurous, whatever the outcome. And even if it doesn't work out quite as you had hoped, then the fact that you took action in the first place and had the courage to take on one of life's greatest challenges will have earned you the right to feel proud of yourself because you did something many others were too afraid to do. And this in itself sets you above those others and will rightly increase your confidence.

Making a movie about your success

The chances are that you will succeed and the rewards will feel a hundred times greater when that happens. A method for giving you confidence is to visualise and feel, with all your senses, the movie of you having achieved success and how you see that. This could be your first big contract, the first time the money appears in your bank account, the wonderfully strong relationship you have with an important client, the lifestyle it allows you and the feeling it gives you every day knowing that you have pulled off something you hadn't imagined you could, despite the challenges and any setbacks. You will see yourself walking tall, laughing, feeling confident, relaxed, positive and capable, and you will envisage people liking and admiring you and wanting to do business with you. You will play out the words used, the facial expressions, sounds, sensations and feelings, and that will reinforce your belief in yourself that will enable you to take action and start your business and succeed.

REAL LIFE STORY

Anja was born in East Germany, thinking she would never be allowed to leave the country and travel. After the Wall came down she got a job and started travelling and moving between countries. She has lived in the USA, Ireland and now the Netherlands. She started her business after doing something she loved while working for someone else.

'I never wanted to become a manager because I thought it meant controlling people and bossing them around. Then I got promoted and noticed I could coach my team members rather than control them. After a while I started coaching my manager colleagues as well and then I had the idea for the People Management coaching cards. This year I'm going to give workshops at a university, never having studied at a university myself,' said Anja.

The People Management coaching cards I created practically started my business. I was still employed when I created them. Then one customer who bought them asked what else I could do for them and suddenly I was a consultant and coached their managers. Now I am a full-time coach and recognised professional.

'I've had to overcome lots of things during the start-up phase of my business, but I noticed action inspires and experience brings confidence. In my case, having it done it at least once equals having experienced it. Whatever it is – stating my prices, providing some new training or a coaching programme, coaching my first individual client – it is something I never thought I could do. And now I love it. I might be nervous doing things the first time, but once I can say "I've done it before", my confidence increases.

'As for changes: my business grows when I allow myself to do things that I thought I couldn't do. The standards I set myself are way too high and people are perfectly happy with the results even if I think they could have been better. But I'm a big fan of 'being comfortable' because that's when we are authentic and ourselves.

'What prompts me to change? Depending on what it is, the feeling of having no other option, the feeling of not being able to forgive myself if I don't do it or the chance to achieve what I want in a more comfortable way that agrees with my values,' added Anja.

REAL LIFE STORY

Cheryl Bigus' restaurant business venture 'failed miserably' 13 years ago. She felt shame and guilt over the failure. The shame was because of the size of the failure, and also because there were rumblings among her peers who were cynical and made unflattering comments about her business efforts. She felt guilty because of the family money she lost in the effort, which is something she regretted for many years. She felt stagnant and hid professionally for years before finally accepting what had happened and feeling proud for trying. Cheryl then learned to build her shattered confidence.

'First, I try to exercise and have positive physical movement every day. If it isn't a formal workout, I at least walk the dog. Deep breathing and moving the blood is the most positive reinforcement. Second, I remind myself that if I am authentic in my thoughts and actions I can be proud of what I am trying to accomplish. I now have children and I look at them every day and show them through example that you can learn and strike out on your own at any age. I want to set a great example for them and this moves me forward every day. I also have my husband who is the greatest support to me. Having him and his encouragement in my life gives me confidence and motivation,' said Cheryl.

'I realised a few years back that if I don't second guess my first instincts, or let the cynics get to me, and if I go for my goals, I get them accomplished. I remind myself every day that I am authentic and an individual, and very well informed on my chosen area of expertise, and with that comes confidence. I approach every day in a manner in which I know, at the end of it, I will have learned something. No matter how good I am at something, I don't let the ego get out of hand; I approach things with the intent to educate, but also to learn. Defining my goals in this way gives me internal peace and boosts my confidence.

'I overcame serious anxiety and self-doubt through time and patience. For a long time after my restaurant failure, I was plagued with doubt, but as people came to me for my expertise in food and natural health, my confidence slowly recovered. I still have self-doubt (who doesn't), but now I don't let it stop me from moving forward.

'If I was to counsel someone who lacks confidence, I would tell them to write down their big goal. Then below that write down the steps it would take to get there and then below that categorise each one in order of priority. Then break out those tasks into monthly, weekly and then daily tasks in order to get the person on the path to accomplishing their goals. Before they know it, they are on their way to fulfilling their dream. When they look back and see progress, this automatically builds confidence. This can be done with everything from house chores to starting a business,' she added.

Chapter 6

Confidence for non-work life situations

Even though in our life outside work we should feel freer to be ourselves and to be the person we want to be, in a way that our working life doesn't always allow, too many of us still let our confidence levels adversely affect what we achieve personally. And this in turn also affects our working life. Even when we're not at work, we can still feel inhibited by process and protocol as well as other people and our own perceptions about ourselves.

Pigeonholing

Most of us have an unhealthy obsession with and an everyday habit of pigeonholing people both personally and professionally. But as much as this may give us a superficial sense of reassuring context, this internal analysis of others can not only be misleading, it can also inhibit our ability to communicate confidently and effectively in both our working and non-working lives. Pigeonholing people into neat little boxes will invariably also contain and constrict our own opportunities, from getting better paid to finding and developing great friendships.

This is because pigeonholing only takes into account what people appear to have or who they appear to be, not necessarily what the real story is. It takes time and insightful communication to really understand the depth and breadth of someone. But the pace of modern society doesn't always allow us to take this time and also to weigh up the many varied facts that exist and that we can have at our disposal.

Our pigeonholing processes are, amongst other things, prompted by emotional, professional, personal, cultural and financial uncertainties and insecurities that are induced by a fear of the unpredictable and the unknown, all of which can leave us overwhelmed. We like easy labelling because it feels safe and manageable. But this doesn't give us the full picture as people are naturally diverse and complicated.

For instance, very few shoppers avidly read the labels on jars and packets at supermarkets as we tend just to consider what the contents look like and what the main descriptive caption says. But, using the same analogy, if we don't examine people properly, quickly pigeonholing them instead, then we're not likely to find out until it's too late that some turn out to be organic and others full of E numbers, the latter of which won't be good for us.

There are so many ways we can be pigeonholed in terms of where we live, the car we drive, the people we hang out with and the person we marry, our employment sphere, our job title, our income and even what we wear.

Pigeonholing people is invariably personally and professionally limiting for those you're trying to box up and package and, as a result, for you too. Why limit your ability – or that of others, for that matter – to live a life with unlimited possibilities and to engage with all that others might open up for you in different parts of your life by restricting your inner communication with yourself as well as what you communicate to others?

In short, pigeonholing others pigeonholes you by how you interact with those you pigeonhole … as a pigeonholer. That's one hell of a lot of pigeonholing. So much so, it's enough for you to want to break free and open up your mind to others' infinite variety and, just as importantly, yours too in a pigeonholing-free world. And this will enable you to feel and be more confident and to open up your life to opportunities and experiences that will further enrich your self-worth and self-belief.

Perception is projection

Think about how you appear to someone else in your present state and how your lack of confidence will come across. Their instinct about you will be guided by how you feel about yourself. Perception is projection. So if you feel and therefore act in an unconfident manner, you will come across as unconfident. As a result, people will react to you accordingly and are less likely to buy into you.

Ask yourself what you don't feel you're confident about. Say it's because you've told yourself that you're no good at mixing with people you don't know at a party. Why do you believe that is the case? The simple answer is that you, like millions of others, have felt or feel shy about going up to chat to someone you don't know, certainly if they appear more confident than you. But, just imagine how you will feel when you pluck up the small amount of courage required to talk to someone and they're delighted that you did so. This is unless you go up to them only to grin awkwardly, or even inanely, and look as if you're struggling to form a word or remember your own name.

The irony is that we do things every day of our lives which at one point we found too difficult or overwhelming to do, from walking and riding a bicycle to mental arithmetic and even performing the natural and the necessary on the toilet. We had to keep trying after we failed and we got there. You managed it back then so you now have the chance to move on to other useful skills, like talking to people, which we are all more than capable of doing, certainly with more experience and a greater range of abilities that we aquire through life.

Some try to appear confident with less than nonchalant nonchalance. This is to cover up the fact that they don't feel at ease with themselves and/or the situation. Others come across as arrogant and this will alienate those they inflict their clumsy coping behaviour on because they are made to feel inadequate and/or dismissed. Ironically, by being natural and allowing others to see you as less confident people are more likely to warm to you and, in so doing, give you the belief and therefore the confidence you need. This in turn will give you more reason to be more sure of yourself.

Talking to people you don't know

99% of people are missing out on making a better impression, improving their career prospects and even appearing more attractive because of one simple communication flaw that has been programmed into us, often unwittingly. And this is down to people feeling they don't have the confidence to do an everyday task, namely talking to a human being.

When we meet someone, certainly for the first time, whether in a professional or personal capacity, what we tend to do is start thinking and then acting as 99% of people do. The thinking involves the following kind of thoughts:

■ How does my voice sound?

■ How do I come across – happy, sad, tense, clueless, competent, unintelligent, confident, nervous, angry, disinterested, interested?

■ Are my clothes all right?

■ Do they like me as a person?

■ Is my attitude appealing?

■ What will happen and where will this go or not go? And why?

■ What can I do about it if none of the above is right?

■ Does the Queen have moments like this?

■ Should men cleanse, tone and moisturise?

Depending on your answers – unless of course you're the Queen or, as a man, you're a little too in touch with your feminine side – you can then act in some of the following ways:

■ Sound unsure of yourself.

■ Appear tense, clueless, unintelligent, disinterested and nervous.

■ Fidget with and adjust different parts of your clothing.

■ Call the Queen.

■ As a man, inexplicably apply some face cream.

This happens (well, the first three points) all the time because 99% of people are simply wrapped up in themselves when they communicate because they doubt themselves. And that comes across unconsciously to those you are addressing.

How the clever 1% communicate

The clever and effective 1% of people think the following about the other person:

- What is THEIR voice conveying?

- What is THEIR body language saying about them and how THEY feel?

- How do THEY come across – happy, sad, tense, clueless, competent, unintelligent, confident, nervous, angry, disinterested, interested?

- Are THEY comfortable with their attire?

- Do THEY like themselves as a person?

- Is THEIR attitude appealing to them and others?

- What do THEY want to happen and where do THEY want this to go? And why?

- Do I know someone who knows the Queen's mobile number?

- Why is this man wearing foundation and too much rouge?

Depending on your answers to these questions, you can then adapt your verbal and non-verbal communication to make others feel better about themselves. Listen to what they say and how they say it and pay attention to how they act. This will make them feel special and engaged and engaging, and will make them feel connected to you. It will make them more at ease and more confident.

People are too often wrapped up in themselves. This could be for a variety of reasons: the pressures of work, the need to feel like you can mix it socially with the In Crowd, you're having a bad hair or even a no hair day, or even the fact that your waistline seems to resemble a weather balloon in a strong breeze. By just focusing on you and how you come across – as 99% of people tend to do in personal and even professional situations – you are more likely to draw others' attention to your not so well hidden stress as well as that weather balloon midriff you may or may not have.

But if you focus on the other person, you will not only make them feel better about themselves, meaning they like you more, they will also be less likely to notice that your stomach could read weather conditions at high altitude. They will instead feel that you are a more contented and confident person – a much more attractive state than that stressed out weather balloon look.

REAL LIFE STORY

For most of her elementary school years, Kirstie was home-schooled and she taught herself. She was raised with two brothers and didn't really get out much with the kids in their neighbourhood. But when the family moved to a different state, her mother put her into a public (state) school.

Kirstie recalled: 'Seeing as I never had much interaction with other people, I was a social recluse. I didn't know how to talk to other kids, and when boys would talk to me or tease me I reacted violently because that's how I acted with my brothers.

'My lack of social skills in my younger years was no problem once I grew into my body in high school. I learned to use make-up to enhance my features and I learned to love myself in a way some women never do. I am beautiful and I know it. I show it and I am not afraid. I took a cheerleading class, and though the sport was not for me I was able to learn how to project myself as an individual and inspire confidence in others as well.

'I'm a simple girl after a simple dream. My life is centred around my future family, once it gets started. I'm 20 years old and in the military. I have met a lot of people with self-acceptance issues that end up turning into an uncontrollable problem, like an eating disorder, alcoholism, drug addiction or anger. Being able to help people love themselves for who they are, and what they look like, makes me feel like I could be saving them from themselves. I've helped friends see how beautiful they are to me and if others don't see that, then those people aren't important,' she added.

Going to a party on your own

Aside from the physical security of being in a group, certainly when you're one of several girls hanging out in a less than salubrious part of town, being in a group can give you a sense of security. But it can also give you a false sense of confidence if you rely too heavily on the gang. You can risk feeling that without having the group around you couldn't possibly go to a party, a pub or a nightclub on your own.

How to draw people to you

But ask yourself what will happen if you turn up on your own because some of your friends have cried off, overslept, got lost, had a hair crisis or because they feel just as nervous as you and decide to stay in. Imagine yourself arriving and the front door is opened with a wave of intense chatter complemented by equally animated music, or all that dies as you walk in because it's a more restrained or even boring affair.

How would you like to react? What would you think of someone who looked like a startled kitten thrown into the middle of the local dogs' home at feeding time? Conversely, what would you think of someone who smiled, stood and walked tall, and looked calm, warm and happy? You'd want to talk to the second person, but you would not feel a great urge to rush up to the first person because you'd think of them as unengagingly apologetic and therefore uninspiring and not that attractive.

Now, the self-assured person who appears more confident may be pedalling like mad underneath as everyone stares at them, but they determine that they will believe in themselves enough to stand at a doorway, smile and walk a few yards looking as if they are pleased to be there and meet the people already in the room. Remember that people are drawn to those who appear engaging and genuinely at ease with themselves.

As the brain is programmed to respect authority, try this exercise the next time you step out of a lift or a busy underground train and there's a crowd of people waiting to enter. Before you walk forward, pause and stand in the doorway for slightly longer than they would expect you to. Those gathered in front of you are likely to part, allowing you to move on without being jostled. This is because you are showing that you have a confident authority, which their subconscious minds are telling them to obey.

REAL LIFE STORY

Richard Reed is one of the founders of Innocent Drinks, a highly successful and well known UK-based company, founded in 1999, whose primary business is producing smoothies and flavoured spring water.

Their products are sold in supermarkets, coffee shops and various other outlets nationally as well as in Ireland, the Netherlands, Germany, France, Austria, Belgium, Denmark and Switzerland. Innocent has a 71% share of the £169 million UK smoothie market and the company sells two million smoothies per week.

And yet, despite all this seamless success, Richard admits to never having been a confident person and to often feeling more anxious and shy than confident.

Innocent was founded by Richard and two Cambridge University friends when they were working in consulting and advertising.

In the summer of 1998 when they had developed their first smoothie recipes, but were still nervous about giving up their proper jobs, they bought £500 worth of fruit, turned it into smoothies and sold them from a stall at a little music festival in London.

They put up a big sign saying 'Do you think we should give up our jobs to make these smoothies?' and put out a bin saying 'YES' and a bin saying 'NO' and asked people to put their empty bottles in the bin they thought most appropriate. At the end of the weekend the 'YES' bin was full, so they went in the next day and resigned.

On its first day of trading, April 28, 1999, the business sold 24 smoothies. This week alone, it will sell about two million. They have sold a small stake in their company to Coca-Cola for £30 million.

'The reality is that I can be pretty sensitive and feel insecure at times and certainly shy. I was this kid who, every Sunday, at the Sunday lunch dinner table, would absolutely, for no rhyme or reason, burst into tears, every Sunday, like clockwork. My parents couldn't understand it. I couldn't understand it. I just felt so sad and anxious.

'There was one time when my father suggested I go on a caving trip. I think he was trying to "man me up" a bit. I think I was nine at this point.' Richard didn't want to go and then, from nowhere, decided that he was going to force himself to make the trip. He reflects that, amazingly, 'I came back with an absolute obsession for caving. I couldn't have loved it more. And then, poor Dad, he had to pay for me to go caving for the next 10 years!

'I think people look at me and think "That guy is so confident." But actually I feel anxious more often than I feel confident. But it ebbs and flows. And I've found the best cure for anxiety is to just get on with things. I have increased my confidence by literally forcing myself into situations that felt uncomfortable but that ultimately I've coped with and sometimes enjoyed.

'You can actually force yourself from a negative thought into a positive thought. You can choose to think positively. You can choose to think negatively. It's a choice. I know that's easy to say and I know there are a whole load of issues to go through to make that the reality. But I do know that fundamentally, at its deepest level, it is a choice to say that, just for now, just for this second, I am going to think the positive version of that thought.

'People think that if they're thinking negatively, that must be truer than if they think positively. But the reality is that the negative and positive interpretations of the same event are equally true. It's not like negativity has got the monopoly on truth. You take the same fact and can view it negatively or positively. Why not try it from the positive side rather than the negative side. It makes life just so much more enjoyable!

'Don't buy into the myth that there are some rules. There aren't. No one is any better or any worse than anyone else. It comes down to this: that if you've got something you want to do then do it. Accept the fact, because you are a human being, that you will have with you, as a constant presence, your negative side, sitting on your shoulder and whispering: "You're not good enough", "It's not for you", "You can't do it and even if you did it, it would fail".

'You will hear those voices, but you just have to understand that every single other human being hears those voices too. You've just got to rip them off and throw them down and squash them under your foot and accept the fact that the next day you'll be back there again. Don't wait for the voices not to be there.

'Accept that the voices are there. You've just got to realise that it's part of you, and it's not the better part of you. It just makes you human. But keep getting back to what it is you want to do and follow that and make sure you are marshalling your time and energy to achieve that.'

Asking someone out

There are two sets of advice here: one for men and one for women.

Men asking women

It's easier for men to ask women out rather than the other way round because that's what society is used to. It's harder for a woman to ask a man out because, in simplistic terms, that's like the hunted hunting the hunter. And not all hunters know how to deal with that. Having said that, it makes a woman appreciate what men go through. And it isn't always easy, is it!

You need courage, first and foremost, along with belief, determination, action, resilience and a sense of humour. The best way to engage a woman is to be yourself – unless of course you've got the sort of personality that would do justice to her image of a homicidal tin pot dictator without conversation skills and, worst of all, without a sense of humour.

Start with a smile

So many chat-up lines are, for the most part, corny and crass and go down as well as a burst of flatulence at a funeral. Counterproductive and embarrassing. So start with a smile – not a nervous I feel like I'm about to do a base jump with only a pair of granny's old bloomers strapped to my back look – and a hello. She will have already made a variety of judgements about you before you've even opened your mouth. But we all do that, so don't even give it a second thought. You're doing the same with her.

You can begin with a comment – this could be something general or even light-hearted or off the wall – or an open question. Women are used to asking men questions and letting them talk, in fact so much so, that a lot of men just seem to run out of time when it comes to talking about the woman as well! Have some staple questions that can get the conversation off to a start. Don't make them intrusive. I hear some crackers from time to time and included in the Not To Use style book are:

■ 'Shall we compare net worths?'

■ 'Have you shaved your legs?'

■ 'Would you like a naughty fleshy experience?!'

These have all been used in the heat of social battle. The men concerned are, at last count, still single! I could write a book on this subject alone, but this one is about keeping things simple and practical. You can actually have the guts to go up to a woman you like the look of, you can make her smile or laugh when you open your mouth with a thought-provoking question or a witty one-liner and engage her in easy conversation and even get a date out of her, or whatever you both finally have in mind, but it all boils down to one thing.

The power of naturalness

Naturalness is one of the most under utilised but most attractive personal traits. If you are yourself, people sense it and are more likely to be at ease with you because they are also more likely to feel at ease with themselves. That way you're more likely to appear relaxed. And when you're relaxed you're not going to come across as someone who's desperate to make the emotional or social sale, as it were. That will just deter the woman you're trying to communicate with because you'll go into the social fray armed to the teeth with your supposedly devastating seduction arsenal and strategies. She'll counter-attack with anything from a withering look to something more robust and rejecting. You'll feel like a fool, certainly if this is witnessed by others, and your confidence will be dented. And that's that. You'll be out of action while you go and have your emotional wounds attended to.

If you are your own person then you put less pressure on yourself than if you are trying to be something you think others want you to be at that moment. If you do try to be someone other than who you really are, you will appear desperate to be liked. That can come across subliminally as a little needy, and neediness isn't attractive. If you appear to be someone who is happy just to let the moment take its natural path then the other person is much more likely to feel at ease with this and therefore you – however it turns out.

Women asking men

As cultural convention dictates that, generally speaking, it's men who ask women out and not the other way round, it takes courage for a woman to ask a man. It also takes belief and the right sort of action, but not necessarily persistence. This is because men can find women asking them out a little disconcerting as men see themselves as the hunters and not the hunted! It obviously depends on what you're asking the man out for – or even asking him in for.

If you're inviting him to a party you're organising, that's less personal and pressured and more open, so it's easier because he isn't going to see himself being pinned down to something with just one woman. But, interestingly, if it's for a night of room-shuddering – and certainly no strings attached – sex then this is likely to be easier than asking a man out on a get to know you (with your clothes on) date. Put very simply, men can deal more readily with physical rather than emotional intimacy in the immediate to short term. But, for whatever purpose, if you are going to ask a man out then your self-confidence is key.

There are three ways to ask a man out and to grab his attention in the hope that he might flirt back or even feel comfortable enough to ask you out. And only one of them really works.

There's the purring, smouldering Bond Girl Baddy 'do as I tell you or I'll pickle your bits' approach. This vampish, almost vixen-like way of terrifying your way into a man's affections can work on the wrong type of guy if the woman and the guy want the wrong sort of post-purr activity. But a decent guy, no matter how pneumatic a woman appears, is just going to think she is overdoing it and hamming it up to the point that it's a mixture of the funny and fearsome. At best it will lead to something short–term.

There is something refreshing about being direct and up front about what you want to happen, certainly when it involves something quite intimate. Having said that, the way you say it is important. I remember being in a nightclub in Swansea in Wales when two women sidled up to me by the side of the dance floor and one of them asked with a deadpan, the-paint-has-yet-to-dry tone, 'Have you got an erection?' I didn't have and her uninspired approach and manner didn't inspire a surge in the trouser department either. And she had no follow-up. It was like she hoped it would lead to great things without her having to do anything. She was lost for words and I was lost for excitement.

Then there's the frightfully apologetically nice and fumbling approach, complete with uneasy attempts at humour and conversation, complemented by plenty of equally awkward silences, just like that wonderful scene in Four Weddings and a Funeral where the Hugh Grant character runs after the Andie MacDowell character to tell her in a beautifully bumbling and bashful British way that he loves her, only to then tell her she probably isn't interested, such is his insecurity and lack of confidence.

There are lots of truly lovely women, who would and will make great partners, who scupper their chances of inflaming a man's innermost feelings because they come across with little to no self-belief. (And self-belief and a warm confidence are very attractive.) This is the sort of woman you want to put your arm around and tell her everything will be okay, before sending her off to mum to have a heart-to-heart and a cup of hot cocoa.

Being your warm self

The third way is the easiest. It's about being natural, being oneself and being just as much at ease as a woman is with her friends. The woman in option 1 wants to dominate the man – but apart from some bored

company directors and politicians who pay for this sort of stuff, many guys don't like to be dominated completely by a woman, certainly not an alpha male. The woman in option 2 acts as if she could easily be dominated by a man and puts them on a pedestal of sorts. The woman who is going to grab a man's attention, both physically and emotionally, is the one who is herself, the one who's congruent and is not afraid to be – and this is important – her normal kind, warm, genuine, clever, funny, adventurous self.

There's something very alluring about a woman who's not afraid to be naturally sensual (men are physical and sexual beings and this counts for a lot) and feminine, but who isn't afraid to hold her own in conversation with a man so she makes him feel that she is an equal. Naturalness is one of the first and most important victims in the dating scene, certainly among the more professional and urban set whose personal brand can sometimes focus more on appearing to be something they think members of the opposite sex will like because it looks good in films and in Sex and the City.

The woman who a real man will be interested in is the one who doesn't try too hard because she's just being herself – and that takes confidence which is attainable – and who has an air of reconciliation and self-acceptance about her. This will put him at ease because, despite outer appearances prompted by male pride and ego, men are not always as relaxed and confident on the inside as they might appear. Remember, the man is used to hunting and most like to. And the woman who he sees as he surveys the emotional and social savannah has got to be appealing enough to get his attention.

Dealing with rude, bitchy and patronising people

Potent politeness and put-downs

The first thing to remember is that if someone is being hostile then you have somehow rattled the cage of this unhappy creature. It shows you affect and unsettle them. This could be because they are jealous in some way. For instance, you may usually make people feel good whereas this person, because they are patronising and snide, may not

have this kind of effect on others. This may confound them and they take out their frustration on you. Alternatively, they may be having a bad day or a bad month or two and you just happen to be there at the wrong time.

Now, some might argue that someone's unpleasantness may be due to the fact that you deserve it because of some character or other flaw of yours. But, if that were the case, would a confident and right-thinking person resort to acting like the person they think is bitchy, rude or patronising? No they wouldn't because a confident person doesn't need to justify themselves by trying to put down someone else in an unpleasant way. They know they're happy with themselves no matter what they are called. My father is an excellent example of this as his self-belief and quiet confidence completely take the sting out of any verbal attack. If someone tries to be rude to him, he just feels sorry for them thinking, 'Poor soul. They must be most unhappy or unwell!'

Another option is to question, with a calm, smiling kindness, what they're hoping to achieve by acting in that way, even adding that the offender seems intent on trying to make a point without actually attempting to win over their audience which all seems rather pointless.

The third option is the good old put-down. Again, this must be said with warmth so that you don't come across as acidic as the person who has been rude to you. Comedians have put-downs rehearsed and ready to deliver when members of their audience heckle them or worse. You must practise saying these put-downs with a well-timed calmness and a tone that gives the impression that you're not fussed about putting them in their place. Obviously things can escalate, certainly when ego kicks in.

Maintaining your dignity

Always retain your composure. To help with this, imagine how you would feel if you were being rude to someone and they treated you as above. Play in your mind a movie of this situation. As you become more defensive and spiky with that person, those around you, including the person you patronised or were spiteful towards, would look at you as if you were someone they had started to think less of and didn't want around. You would feel isolated and your increased lashing out at their quietly confident reaction to you would make you feel more isolated and, in truth, more unhappy with yourself.

You don't want to be like this kind of person and will not be. You want to be the one who maintains their dignity, the one who either smiles at the insulter with pitying amusement or cleverly puts them in their place without losing their cool. You are more than likely to take the sting out of their attack and, in a form of verbal aikido, use their force and momentum against them. It's about taking the right action that befits your personality and being resilient enough and believing in yourself enough to know that you are so much better than the person the insulter tries to make you feel while, ironically, it is they who are the sort of person they try to make others out to be.

Dealing with critical partners and family members

This can be one of the most destabilising aspects of our lives. Our partner and our family should be our nucleus, a sacred refuge from the rigours of life. But that is not always the case. A criticism or negative experience or a set of them with a parent, in particular, feels about ten times worse than if it was from someone outside the family. This is because we want to believe in the sanctity of our family, those we are the genetic product of and therefore are meant to be closest to emotionally. But that is no guarantee of familial harmony.

How To Help Yourself Take Action

The reason a partner, parent or sibling is critical or dismissive is not the most important aspect. It's how you deal with it. The confidence you must develop in a situation where you are increasingly at destabilising odds with your loved one must be dug up from within with the help of good friends and supportive and trusted associates. It will take time and there could well be setbacks. You must not put pressure on yourself to pretend that you feel great in the face of family conflict. That will increase the stress on you.

Taking the fundamental pillars of confidence, covered at the start of this book, you will increase your belief in yourself through resilience and determination to see the criticisms for what they are. You will also persist in working at reinforcing your own self-belief, with regular positive self-affirmations and the courage to stand up to the truly unfair criticisms.

Remember, a parent is there to support and guide you from a young age. When you're very young, this will mean praising you as well as telling you off. But there must be a balance. Alas, there are so many instances when this just doesn't happen because the parent concerned may not have dealt with their own demons that they've allowed to adversely affect their own personality and parenting.

This behaviour can be continued in partnerships by people who are critical in the same way their parents and even a sibling have been with them. They take this out on the person closest to them – their partner – as a means of trying to even up the score. It's a way of attempting to dilute the insecurities and other negative guff that they endured when younger because they haven't yet dealt with it and moved on from there, even though they need to exorcise their private demons.

Always Having a Choice

But we have a choice as to how we deal with this. We can try to help the other partner as practically as possible and, after a determined effort on your part, you then have the choice to walk away. Sometimes the very thought of that is the catalyst for the critical one to make a significant change in their behaviour. One should take confidence from the fact that we have choices – not always the easiest to make – but they are choices all the same.

REAL LIFE STORY

Nesta Wyn Ellis comes across as a very strong, determined, capable and confident woman. But she understands the loss of confidence many women suffer because of the relationships they have with their partners. Nesta, who wrote a biography of the former British Prime Minister John Major, was a confident and successful child because she was always encouraged. But, as an adult, her confidence was severely affected by a bad relationship.

'I too have experienced that and know just what it's like when your confidence is undermined by being told you're wrong each time you take a decision or make a choice in your career or life. It's awful when you have no one else to reinforce your self-confidence, certainly if a partner uses various methods to prevent you making or meeting your own friends,' she said.

Nesta returned to the UK and began to see a hypnotist to restore her self-confidence. It worked and she went on to achieve considerable success as a journalist and as an author. She is now also developing a career as a singer and songwriter.

'Everyone needs success to reinforce their inner confidence in their own abilities and judgement. If you lack confidence it means you have had bad experiences when you have made decisions or chosen a path. The trick is not to be a perfectionist because you may demand too much of yourself. If you are trying to achieve self-confidence give yourself points for even small successes,' said Nesta.

'Are you successful at getting people to like you? Are you successful at being patient? Are you successful at giving love (that's a very undervalued gift)? Are you successful at choosing the best eating regime for yourself? Are you successful at picking out attractive clothes? Are you successful in doing what you say you will do? All these are seemingly small things, but if you build on these small beginnings in evaluating your successes you can gradually extend them to bigger things. It's really a case of building your character up from the ground. Slow, but eventually it works.

'I've learned that too many people are jealous of a successful person and that means a self-confident person too. One has to know what one is good at and what one does less well. Then, by focusing on the things you are good at, make opportunities for yourself and eventually you will succeed. Then your self-confidence will be enhanced. It's best to know yourself very well, your strengths and weaknesses included. Then you can evaluate yourself and award yourself points for achievements in different areas of life. That will give you self-confidence in those areas.'

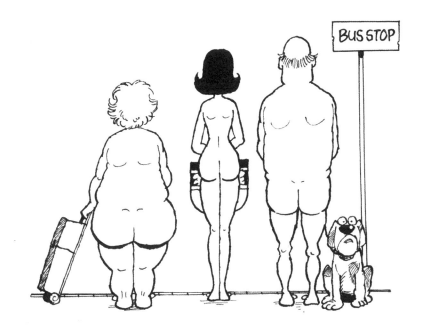

Feeling good naked

Accept yourself

Your confidence will determine how good you look in the buff. If you feel that you don't look good when naked that is how you will come across because what you perceive about yourself is what you project to the outside world. Very few people have perfect natural bodies and, even then, most of the people who many of us think of as being blessed with them believe they are imperfect. No matter how beautiful or handsome you are there always seems to be a reason to find some fault with ourselves, no matter how small. So, take the pressure off yourself and learn to accept yourself as you are.

Staying in shape

That said, the more you look after your fitness and diet, the better you're going to feel about yourself because you will look more appealing without any clothes on, as well as with them on. Alas, too many people just don't make much of an effort to stay in shape. Although, having said that, round is a shape, if not quite the look that will help you feel good in your birthday suit. So, if you're lazy, don't eat well, munch huge mountains of food, particularly the unhealthy stuff, and don't exercise, then you're more likely to waddle than waft. You'll also be more self-conscious about the increasing gulf between the person you are and the person you'd like to look and feel like.

To keep in shape, you need the determination to take action and persist in making yourself fitter and leaner. As research has shown, the more physically attractive you are, as a man or a woman, the more likely you are to be successful both professionally and personally. That will help your confidence and when the time comes to get naked – and there could well be more suitable offers-cum-chances to do so! – then you're going to feel a lot better.

Attitude Makes Imperfections More Attractive

On a psychological level, even if you looked like you had swallowed a minibus, but you still loved who you were and carried yourself accordingly, then you would become more attractive than if you acted as if you were physically unappealing. A classic case in point is the nude models who pose for art students. I've seen a few and they are, for the most part, very generously proportioned. Do they care? No. Not a jot. Otherwise why would they pose nude, and not always in the most relaxed or dignified of positions, in front of men and women who then spend hours scrutinising their every curve, crevasse and curl. The reality is that no one in such scenarios cares that one of them is naked. Everyone just gets on with it.

Unless you're going to streak at some major sporting event – why is it never a political event? – then the chances are you're only going to be seen by very few people. So you have to like you or, at least, be determined to make yourself into a better naked specimen that you like. Then, there's your partner.

Hopefully, he or she or, if you can't remember because of a varied love life, both he and she will still like seeing you naked. But remember the chances are that they might also have concerns about being naked and could well feel the same as you. But, say they no longer feel the same flutter of excitement when they see you in the nude and you sense this. If you react to this negatively and allow your confidence to be dented, then you will compound their view in both your minds and this will further affect your feelings about yourself and theirs too. And so it goes on.

Make a habit of repeating to yourself verbally or in written form the things about your body that you do like. This could be from the way you walk and your posture to the fullness of your lips to the alluring twinkle in your eyes. You need to regularly remind yourself of what makes you attractive when you're naked. The more you do this the more you are likely to realise you have something to feel really good about your body. And that, in turn, will improve your self-esteem and your self-confidence when you're clothed.

Because we're bombarded by beauty and physical perfection – even when it hasn't been airbrushed in a magazine – it's very easy to think we fall short and that we can never live in the hallowed world of the models and others who are presented as paragons of physical delight. Not only do they not always stay like that, but what they have to go through to maintain their look is as challenging as it is restricting. But, above all, the thing that makes people attractive is how they feel about themselves.

The size 16 woman can be a lot sexier than the size 8. This could be because the former is more accepting than the latter who can fret constantly about putting on weight and losing her looks. The larger woman realises that she wants to rely on more than her physical appearance and therefore adds another dimension to her character. That gives her more substance and that can give her more confidence, which will help her feel better about herself physically.

REAL LIFE STORY

Caprice Bourret is an American lingerie supermodel, actress, television personality and businesswoman and has been one of the most photographed women in the world. The former Wonderbra model has appeared on more than 300 magazine covers.

She was voted GQ magazine's Woman of the Year and Maxim's International Woman of the Year for three consecutive years. She has featured in television ad campaigns for Diet Coke and Pizza Hut and has appeared on numerous TV programmes. In 2006, she invested her own money to launch what is now a successful business, selling lingerie, swimwear and homeware. But her beauty and her famous body have been as much of a blight as they have been a blessing.

'Confidence is crucial; but there is a difference between confidence and arrogance. Arrogance is all ego and that's a disaster,' said Caprice.

'Half the battle is mental, feeling you are confident and that you can actually accomplish what you want. It's about keeping on going until you achieve your end result. It could be anything in life. It could be a job, a relationship or a personal goal. And when you come across obstacles you get your tushy back up and keep going. There is no such word as "no". There are solutions and "yes I can".

'I'm an American and I was raised by my mom to believe I could be whatever I wanted to be so I could go out there and attain anything I desired. The thing I find in England, in particular, is that there is an echelon system where, if you're in one bracket, then you're made to believe you can't make it to the next bracket.

'Of course I've had very bad times in my life when I lacked confidence. I remember I kind of went into a hole and went through a little bit of a depression. That was about 2005. There were a multitude of things that happened in my personal life.

'I was caught drink-driving in 2005 and was subsequently banned from driving for 12 months.

'It was made very public and I was publicly disgraced and humiliated – deservingly so – and that just catapulted me into a number of disasters in terms of relationships and other things. It was an emotional whirlwind and I spiralled downwards. I couldn't get myself back up for months. Then I started getting into meditation and it changed my life.'

'To those who don't have the background, the brains, the beauty, the body, the bank balance, the back-up and other advantages, Caprice admitted that 'I didn't always have the brains! I never went to university. I had a private high school education and called it a day as I had to make money.

'A lot of my success now is down to my researching and teaching myself. You can't be lazy. You've got to do the work. I work my 12-hour days. I'm constantly working. I'm on holiday and I'm still working. I go to sleep at night and I'm still working. I wake up at 7 o'clock in the morning and I'm still working.

'I didn't know anything about the underwear business. I was a model, for goodness sake! And I taught myself and learned through my mistakes.

'In some respects I have been very blessed. But in other respects I really have to look after myself. I would love to sleep in an extra three hours every morning, but I don't. I get my tushy up between 6.30am and 7.00am and I go and work out, as I gain weight just by looking at food. The rest of my family are very voluptuous. There are big genes in my family and I have to work my tushy off as it doesn't get any easier the older you get.

'I am always dieting. Always. I watch what I eat. I live for watching what I eat. I can't stand it. I loathe it. But this is my life. Now, if you saw me in the morning you would probably be horrified. When I go out at night and you see me in newspapers and magazines, that's the result of an hour of putting on make-up. That's me doing my hair treatments once a week. It's about really looking after myself. I take 51 vitamins a day.

'You can always make yourself look better, regardless of genes. Everything is work. If you want to look better, you have to work at it. When I started my underwear business, I learned everything about it. My parents never gave me anything because at 17 I was on my own. I have done everything on my own merit.'

Stereotyping can be a problem. 'Firstly, I was a well known model and, secondly, I'm a woman. That's even worse than being a model! I had to overcome this stereotype and I did. There are some days when it's such a damn drama. It's all too much. But the good news is that tomorrow is a new day with new energy.'

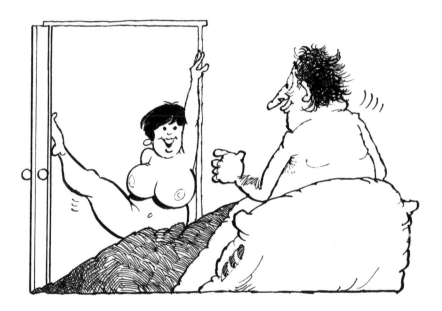

Sexual confidence

Your spirit is more important than your shape

The first thing to remember is that sex is meant to be fun – certainly if it involves another person! – and that it's not meant to be a potentially draining or even damning test of our every gasp, gyration, groan and groin action. So many of us worry, more than we like to admit, about

how we perform and about our physical proportions and appearance. And that can not only reduce our potential pleasure, but, because of this inhibiting mindset, it can also affect the other person's pleasure as you fret and even fumble about – even more than even I usually do!

This is a vast subject, but this book is about distilling everything down into simple and very practical terms to help you with your confidence. The simple answer is that the sexiest thing about a person is their attitude. Their physical attributes can certainly help complement this, but not always. A gorgeous physical specimen without brains, wit, warmth, charm, kindness or confidence is like a beautiful Ferrari or Aston Martin car that drives like a Cold War Trabant or a creaky old three-wheeler. Like the stunning car, the gleaming beauty or hunk will grab your attention, but when you get inside (I'm still using the car analogy here, by the way) or look under the bonnet, it's a huge let-down as there's nothing to sustain that initial visual joy.

The same goes with people. Just because a woman is a beauty with pulsating proportions or a man is knicker-twitchingly handsome with a muscled and toned body to boot, they are not necessarily sexy. Some of the sexiest women I've met are not the prettiest. They didn't have the best skin. They didn't have the best bodies. They didn't have the best hair. But what they did have was spirit and sparkle, drizzled with endless amounts of sensuality.

Some of the world's most beautiful women, women who many imagine can get who they want and have what they want, are and have been some of the most unhappy of people. This is to do with their and other people's expectations of them and the nerve-fraying pressures they sometimes allow themselves to endure. In some cases, it's like they feel they have to maintain the act of the everyday goddess who has a life blessed by beauty and confidence. The sometimes tragic irony is that this is anything but the case.

I have met various women who fit into this category. I remember one very well. She appeared to have everything going for her. She was clever, positive, energetic, with a great sense of fun and an enthusiasm for life. She was also tall with a perfectly toned body with all the right curves, stylish auburn hair and a most becoming smile. She was a very likeable woman in her late twenties. She also had a great job, a lovely house, a sporty car and a loving boyfriend.

Months after I first met her I came across her again. This time, the face that had been so alive and attractive was drained of colour and joy. She was wearing too much make-up and her becoming sense of energy had deserted her. And when we got talking she told me what had happened.

She had had a breakdown. She had been living a lie. The irony was that the person inside was increasingly at odds with the person others saw. They saw perfection. She saw and felt imperfection. She felt that she was trying too hard to be the person everyone admired and begrudged her for, rather than allowing herself to have her off days.

As a result, she told me, she lost her boyfriend, her job, her house, her car and, of course, her confidence. So she changed her life and became more accepting of who she really was and had the courage to do that. This helped her self-belief and this in turn helped her become more resilient. She's now married and a much more confident person.

Don't make sexual performance like a driving test!

So, no matter what people think you've got, it's what you believe you possess that really counts. This woman seemed to have everything, but then felt she didn't. Conversely, there are women who don't have half of what this seemingly lucky girl had, but who have a level of

positive acceptance about them that makes them at ease with who they are. And this makes it easier to feel more sexually confident because, for instance, they can accept that their natural breasts may not point magnetic north, like some of the fake ones do, that their nose is less than dainty or that some of their curves may not be in sync with glossy magazine thinking.

Men also get hung up about their physical appearance and, of course, the size of their manhood – something that is much written and talked about in the media and elsewhere. Being competitive and wanting to secure the best mate, a man will compare himself to others, certainly those who are hailed as the hero of so many women's hearts. Now, you may not look like George Clooney, but you may be witty and knowledgeable. And, as repeated surveys have shown, a man with a great sense of humour and a good brain is very attractive to women. This has a lot to do with the fact that your brain and how it thinks and makes you act is what makes you feel and appear sexy.

An unselfconscious focus on your body and how you come across sexually means that your lover – or even lovers, if timetable and temperament allow! – won't be distracted by any issues that might seep out. You can each focus on the act itself, as well as each other's good points.

Sexual confidence can be affected at any point, whether it is your first time with someone or whether it's with a long-term partner. It's learning to accept that sexually, as in other aspects of your lives, we all have good and bad days. But this shouldn't alter the fact that we have been and will continue to be sexually confident again.

Men are afflicted by sexual confidence just as much as women. One challenge men have is dealing with the apparent responsibility of creating and sustaining sexual pleasure for a woman. But men are generally brought up to believe that the success or otherwise of sex is mostly down to them. We are often made to feel that we have to set the mood, set her pulses racing and then set her on the path to sexual nirvana before letting ourselves go to enjoy our side of the sexual exchange and woe betide any man who doesn't fulfil his quasi-contractual duties in this intimate exchange.

At the end, it can be like waiting for the results of a driving test to try and judge, by her word or facial expression, whether we have passed or failed. Did we perform the three-point manoeuvre satisfactorily, did we put the brakes on too late or even too early, was our positioning just right and did we try and go somewhere we shouldn't have? That's how many men are made to feel. It's not helped by the media who harp on about the importance of male sexual performance and how this can make or break the woman's enjoyment of sex.

But, as all right-thinking women would agree, sex does involve at least two people who both contribute to the joy or otherwise of the occasion. And of course men forget that women can worry just as much about how they appear physically and how they perform sexually. In fact, research has shown that while two-thirds of women are unhappy with their bodies in some way, even though they may have no reason to be, two-thirds of men are happy with their bodies – even if they have no reason to be.

So being sexually confident is about accepting your body as much as your sexual likes and dislikes and focusing on the other person so that, whether your partner is a man or a woman, they won't feel as if they're on a sexual driving test.

Affirm your abundance of attributes

To know why you should be sexually confident, write down a list of all your good points: physical, sexual, emotional and spiritual. These could be things that people have told you about or that you believe are a plus for you. Go on. We're often our harshest critics, so don't be hard on yourself. If you believe or would like to believe that your

Botticelli bottom or your sonorous shrieks are bonuses in your armoury, then so be it.

Repeat them to yourself, out loud ideally, as these positive affirmations will retune your subconscious mind and alter your behaviour and the vibe you give off. This will make you more sexually attractive and therefore help make you more sexually confident. Obviously, vocalising these intimate incantations just before, during or even after sex with someone might freak them out. You never know. Some women do report that, during the height of the sexual frenzy, some men have begged them breathlessly to shout out 'You're the king!' On such an occasion, it's probably better felt than said.

But what if someone makes you feel bad during the flurries of fornication? If you've been your giving, loving, exciting and adventurous self, then firstly, if someone slags you off during or after such a frightful fumble, then you should not doubt yourself, but the other person. Would someone who's kind, giving and confident tell you, for instance, that the only thing missing was a train manual to read why you humped and pumped? Hell, no. They may not say anything, but you can tell from their world-weary look that they've been overcome by a sudden burst of indifference. You may not truly know what emotions they've concealed from you. You may not be in sync with each other on that occasion. You may be on others.

But, whatever happens, you must recall all the good points you have written down – all your positive affirmations that make you know that you are sexually confident. The more you do this, the more at ease you will be.

Physical confidence

Keeping in good health physically and mentally – and they're linked – will make you feel better about yourself and will also lead to people thinking more highly of you. Endless research has shown that people who are in good physical shape and who are more physically attractive get paid more, get asked out more, have more people wanting to be asked out by them, get taken more seriously, have better jobs and a greater sense of well-being and confidence.

Eat well and exercise regularly

Comfort eating is often a recourse for people who don't feel good about themselves. And that in turn leads to more eating as you decide that your 'I look like I swallowed a minibus' image is not a ratings winner and you ram the equivalent of a family vehicle and a few parking machines in the form of food down your gullet. You need to eat well. And it's a discipline that in turn will make you feel better about yourself. But it needs to be complemented by regular exercise.

The endorphins earned from exercise will also improve your state of mind and body. You will therefore give off a certain positive energy and vibe that will be more likely to engage and even attract people. Regular activity has a number of proven, positive physical and, as a result, mental health effects. Vigorous exercise strengthens the heart as a pump, making it a larger, more efficient muscle. Even moderate activity will boost your muscles, increase flexibility, strengthen your bones, make your heart more efficient, reduce fat, increase stamina and, mentally, will help relieve stress and anxiety.

Sadly, there are too many inert and lazy people who think that a diet of daytime TV programmes about how to lose weight by exercising will, by some form of unusual osmosis, somehow help them get fitter. It takes effort and discipline. But it's so easy to get immersed in just the immediate-term feelings derived from comfort eating.

In the short, medium and long term, eating in this way will make you feel much worse physically and mentally – so much so, that it will become increasingly tough to change your eating habits. It will also therefore become harder to get some control over your life to help you take regular or even any exercise. Interestingly, the American Heart Association attributes about 250,000 deaths a year in the US – about 12% of total deaths – to lack of regular physical activity. So you have to take action.

REAL LIFE STORY

Val McLeod took action. Eighteen years ago, she weighed nearly 600lbs (about 270kg or almost 43 stone). She has since lost more than half that weight.

'While I desire to go further with my fitness goals, I have learned to fully embrace the beauty-filled woman that I am,' said Val who has faced a series of challenges that have tested her confidence.

'My message to anyone lacking confidence always begins with helping them to connect to their truest, most fundamental identity. There is much more detail to this process, but knowing your authentic self is the strongest foundation to a life anchored with confidence. I have affirmations all around me. Every day I write something new that declares or demonstrates my success. I envision myself at the pinnacle of success, which motivates me to push, press and persevere toward my greatest potential. I also begin and end each day with a prayer/proclamation of gratitude. Thankfulness clears the pathway to greatness!' she added.

REAL LIFE STORY

Despite being young, Lisa has rheumatoid arthritis and scoliosis and has been operated on 13 times as a result.

'I have scars on my body and my back has two severe curves. It has been really difficult for me to view myself as physically attractive. However, one thing I've learned is that if my physical differences bother someone, they aren't like me at all. If it bothers my friends, then they weren't friends at all and I won't waste any more time on them. If it bothers a boyfriend, he is so not worth my time!' said Lisa.

'The best thing that I have done to sustain my confidence is to stand up for myself. If I'm being mistreated, I find the proper means to speak out for myself. Today, I know that I am a strong young woman. My parents are very proud of me and my boyfriend always comments that one of his favourite things about me is my strength of character and all the things I've overcome.

'As for advice for others: remember that no one else is better than you. We all are born human and die the same. It's your responsibility to do everything you can to be a good person, make good decisions and treat people respectfully, including yourself. If you do that, you have no reason not to be confident.'

Being held at gunpoint

I have been held at gunpoint a few times by angry men in ugly situations. This once happened in the former Yugoslavia during the war there. I was asleep at the time and was prodded with the barrel tip of a Kalashnikov assault rifle. I was confronted with this barrel-chested monster with wild eyes, a snarl and a particularly bad haircut. I felt like trying to placate him by uttering the immortal line: 'Don't shoot – I'm not well!'

He started shrieking at me in Serbo-Croat and called in a colleague who could speak some English. The colleague translated saying that, looking like a nice guy was obviously a deceptive rouse and I was clearly a spy and could therefore be carrying dangerous things, like weapons, in my luggage, and be trying to smuggle them into the country.

They glared at me. And then I realised I had to come clean. They had me. I confessed that buried deep in my rucksack was … in fact … a Jeffrey Archer novel. Understandably, they were horrified I was trying to smuggle something like that into the country. But then I pointed out that what he said was made-up. Don't worry, I said, it's the same with his novels!

Afterwards, I was tried in a court in my absence, sentenced to death in my absence, so I said they could shoot me in my absence.

There was no court appearance or death sentence, but it was a tricky situation. In such situations, depending on the intention of the gunman or gunmen, I made myself suitably and noticeably humble, but not too submissive so they thought I was pathetic. In the case of the Serbian soldier with the AK-47, I smiled gently and warmly hoping it would work, trying to make him feel that I thought he was a friendly guy. Slowly it worked and we were able to start a dialogue and, to cut short a long story of linguistic stumbling and fumbling, I managed to talk my way out of the situation.

Don't provoke the armed person or people by being either defensive or offensive. They're likely to be in a heightened state and your calmness will help reassure them that they have the situation under control and that they aren't going to be forced to do something that could prove fatal to you, or even them.

You have to believe you can deal with them as effectively as possible so that you will survive without anything nasty happening to you. Keep looking for weaknesses on their part, which suggest they may want to let you go or get away from the situation themselves.

Coping with setbacks

Setbacks are inevitable

Setbacks are a part of everyone's life, no matter how famous or successful you are. Accepting that is the first step in building your confidence when something goes awry, whether it's emotional, financial or physical, or something that leaves you feeling like you've been defeated, like you've been put back down. To use the words of Rudyard Kipling from his poem 'If –':

If you can bear to hear the truth you've spoken
Twisted by knaves to make a trap for fools,
Or watch the things you gave your life to broken,
And stoop and build 'em up with worn-out tools;

Trusting your instinct can save your life

No matter how confident you are as a person – and remember that self-confidence is situational and relative and is neither absolute nor final – you cannot always prevent some setbacks from happening. Some things are out of your control. But your belief in yourself can help you deal with it better than if you weren't confident enough. I nearly died doing something that was unlike almost any other challenge I had faced physically and mentally and what saved me was having the confidence to trust my instinct.

I had just collapsed out of sheer physical exhaustion on the icily cold and snow-hardened south face of Carstensz Pyramid, South East Asia's highest mountain and one of the Seven Summits (the highest mountain on each continent). I had been ill and had not slept properly for four days and nights on a mountaineering expedition that was testing my physical and mental toughness, resolve, belief and courage. And yet I wasn't a mountaineer. I was someone who, at just four weeks' notice, was offered a testing and life-changing challenge that was way beyond my technical, physical and mental comfort zone. I was, at best, an irresponsible scrambler.

I had just reached for a hand-hold about 600 feet up into the climb when I heard the frantic cries above me. 'ROCK!' three voices screamed in quick succession before they watched intently to see what the man-size boulder, hurtling in a zigzag fashion in my direction, would do next, along with a whole collection of differently sized rocks which were raining down on my position.

I was clinging to an almost sheer part of the rock face at the bottom of a steep sided, but shallow and oval shaped gully about 25 metres long and about 10 metres wide. When I looked up I remember seeing the large sharp-edged and irregular shaped boulder bouncing first left, before it then quickly diverted to the right, spinning violently as it did so. I can recall it now only in slow motion. In reality, there must have been about two to three seconds to react. We had all been trained to 'melt' into the mountain, tucking our heads and bodies into the rock face, at the spot we happened to be at if there was such a danger. But I ignored those instructions on instinct and watched and waited. That was to save my life.

Just when I thought the boulder was going to pass me to my right – it was, by then, about 10 metres away at the two o'clock position – it swiftly changed direction and headed straight for me. I had less than a second to react. With a mixture of adrenaline and blind hope, I leapt about a yard along the rock face to my left to grab any hand and foothold. I closed my eyes tightly and braced myself for what, in those few crucial moments, I had judged would be a real 'touch and go' situation. It was literally that. The rock rushed just past my head, hitting the top part of my rucksack and right shoulder, before plummeting down the mountain.

Luckily, that section of my pack was empty and almost flat against my back, as it was only half full, and did not give the boulder anything to catch on to and therefore drag me down to an infuriating end. I say infuriating because, after all the effort involved in getting there, I would not actually have reached the 16,502 ft (5,030 m) summit of Puncak Jaya which, at that point, only about 200 people had climbed successfully.

I had survived because I was confident enough to trust my instinct. Being at the bottom of a major rockfall while clinging to a sheer slope, after having earlier collapsed due to exhaustion, is a 24-carat setback and one that was out of my control. But I had to take action, and quickly, to follow my belief that I should ignore my training.

I undertook the climb because I wanted to feel that I was living life and adding another experience to the adventure I have always wanted my life to be. That took action, determination, courage, belief and resilience. But I also thought ahead and imagined how I would feel when I had conquered the summit and how much more confident I would be as a person because I had overcome a variety of challenges to achieve this.

How to Build and Bolster Your Recovery

The same principles apply if you're dumped by your partner or lose your job. Acceptance should kick in if you have deserved this. If you made your partner constantly feel bad, cheated on them or made a pass at their pet or, at work, you only made fleeting appearances at the office, alienated company clients and made a pass at one of their pets, then, quite frankly, you will have to accept that your time was up.

But if you've done none of these things and you are in fact genuinely the wronged person, then you have to put it in a context. Allow yourself some time to feel bad and upset and even angry but, although you need this release valve, the longer you allow it to fester, the longer you will take to reach a stage where you can get a healthier perspective that will help you heal and then overcome a setback. You can't continue to allow yourself to just see and feel the pain and indignity of the episode and place it at the centre of your thoughts and feelings because this will discolour your outlook on life and your confidence levels. And this will adversely affect the other parts of your life that had been enhanced by your improved self-belief. You will have allowed the other person's actions or words to continue to corrode your confidence.

We can often taunt ourselves about a setback, no matter how small, and go over and over again in our minds just how bad it is and how much it has caused us pain and/or frustration. We let these negative voices into our heart and mind despite the fact that you should be like a best friend to yourself. Would you want such a 'friend' in your every waking hour, criticising and taunting you? Of course not! But that's what so many of us do.

Although there's a huge amount you can do on your own to help yourself regain your confidence after a setback, you will need support and emotional and practical backup. You'll need:

- One to three really good, emotionally enlightened and trustworthy friends.

- Someone and/or something to make you laugh.

- A physical change of environment, certainly one that makes you feel relaxed and happy.

Draw up a list of the varying qualities you have and the successes you have had (we've all got them, so no excuses). Carry it around with you to remind you when you feel low and unsure – looking at the considerable list will remind you of all that you have to offer.

> *'I am a person of many gifts and have a lot to offer the world. I have strengths and weaknesses like everyone else and I might have setbacks, but I have had and will have more successes. That's why people love and like me for who I am, just the way I am.'*

Read this out loud at least a couple of times a day for a week, or more if you need it, so it conditions your mind to believe it and act upon it.

Research was carried out with more than 300 undergraduates who were asked to choose an incident in their lives when someone had hurt them in some way and that was still getting to them.

- Group 1 described the event in detail, but were asked to focus on how angry they were and how it had had a negative experience on their lives.

- Group 2 were asked to do the same thing, but focus on the benefits that had flowed from the experience, such as becoming stronger or wiser.

- Group 3 were asked to describe their plans for the next day.

The results showed that spending even a few minutes finding and addressing some benefits from a bad experience or experiences made those in the second group less angry and upset and so they were more forgiving and less inclined to seek revenge.[11]

REAL LIFE STORY

Barbara developed a debilitating handicap that badly affected her dreams of being a singer on Broadway. Her confidence was dented so much that she said: 'I have many times felt inadequate or lesser than others because of a physical weakness and handicap that is not visible to others. My number one battle is with frustration.'

Her husband and son have helped her hugely with diet and a supplement programme in addition to the enormous amounts of emotional support they give her.

'Having the support of others has been the most profound help to overcoming the frustrations. I truly felt alone and overwhelmed. I needed help. Sometimes we need to ask for help. I have never been good at asking for help, but even coming to terms with needing to was significant,' said Barbara.

But she is equally aware that although getting support from others is crucial in times of great need, 'many of us are too easily persuaded and too concerned about our peers. The truth is that we will often live within the expectations of our peers, and that can lead many down the path of mediocrity. Raise your standards. Don't settle.'

Making significant life changes

About a third of us are only living life at 50% of its potential, according to a survey I conducted on confidence. More of us feel that a fear of failure than fear of the unknown is the most significant factor in stopping us from feeling more confident to do the things we want to do and be the people we want to be.

That's why almost half of us believe that confidence can and will completely transform their lives. And as more than three-quarters of respondents agree and strongly agree that confidence is the main contributory factor in achieving success, you know that if you want to make a significant life change it is possible and you will do it – if you believe you can and want to.

Dreaming with hope

Allow yourself to dream and to hope. Let your imagination stride out towards a new view and a new goal. Please don't be an If Only person where you feel you would have been happier and more successful If Only you had done this or said that. There's a wonderful anonymous quote that says:

> 'Hell is the knowledge of opportunity lost: the place where the person you are meets the person you could have been.'

So, whether you have to make a significant change in your life out of choice or because it was forced upon you, firstly try to imagine how good you will feel when you've got through the sometimes unsettling period of adjustment. You will have experienced and therefore achieved something you hadn't thought you could have done. Always play in your mind the movie of you in a new country, living in a new culture, working in a new job, living with a new partner or coping with a changed condition in your health and see, hear, sense and even smell the new life and how you're thriving on it. Feel how much stronger and more confident you now are because you have taken yourself to a new level of life that you and even others had not thought possible.

Sod It! Face It! Do It!

Create and fine-tune the plan and, by taking action, stick to it with determination and belief that will be reinforced when you have seen it through. This takes courage – a sort of Sod It! Face It! Do It! approach.

Ask yourself what you really want to achieve as opposed to what you just want to do. Achieving has a sense of useful purpose to it that isn't always guaranteed by the act of just doing something. So, ask yourself what you want to achieve and how this will change your life and even the lives of others for the better. Will it make you smile and laugh and feel like you have given yourself an even better opportunity and experience? Whether you succeed or fail, will you feel, both during and afterwards, that you are gliding and galloping through life rather than wading through a restricting swamp of frustrated containment and hollow hopes?

The key questions to ask yourself are:

- What would you do if you weren't afraid?

- What would you do if you knew you couldn't fail?

- What will you gain if you succeed?

- What will you lose if you fail?

- How will you look back on your life if you don't try to achieve this?

- How will you look back on your life if you do try to achieve this?

- How will overcoming and succeeding in this challenge make you feel and act?

You must be aware of the consequences of both success and failure. But if you focus on the experience you'll live through and how much you will gain and grow from that, whether you succeed or fail, as well as the future feeling you will have when you have achieved in part or wholly what you wanted, then whichever way you look at it you will have done something worthwhile. That will help give you the courage to not just make the decision to undertake a significant life change, but also the determination and resilience to follow it through because, in the end, it will make you a more confident person if you choose to be so.

I gave up a perfectly good staff job as a TV news correspondent and newsreader. I had a comfortable and varied life, but I wasn't happy. I wasn't being challenged enough professionally and, personally, I was not living in the greatest place to enjoy the breadth of social, cultural and emotional opportunities that I wanted. After many long walks in the soothingly bucolic countryside, letting my imagination and my heart and mind run an assault course of emotions and hopes blended with an optimistic analysis of the financial and other obstacles and opportunities, I decided what I wanted to do and I had to go.

I drew up a plan and a timetable and laid the foundation stones for what I wanted to achieve. I wanted to keep my hand in as a TV and print journalist to earn money, while my main aim was to be a successful novelist, to earn multi-book deals with large advances. I wrote one novel. But there was no advance, no multi-book deal and I wasn't going to be able to live in my country hideaway and pen great tomes from an elegant south-facing study overlooking the beautiful British countryside. I went back to what I knew, wiser and enriched in terms of life experience, if not hard cash.

But I couldn't ignore that although I had decided that being a novelist wasn't for me, because as much as I love writing and being creative, I also love spending time working with people, I still wanted more out of my life than just being a TV and print journalist – no matter how good my job sounded at dinner parties. To my intense frustration I couldn't work out exactly what I wanted to do. I was in a real professional and personal fog for a good year as I agonised over what career and life path I should follow.

In the end, it was my little sister who arranged an appointment with a company of excellent career psychologists in London. I had read articles about them in the national press which told exciting stories about people who had gone in as a frustrated lawyer and come out to be a happier artist or gone in as a time-serving plumber and emerged as a doctor. After a morning of doing a whole stack of psychometric and personality tests – when they found out that I actually had a personality – I had a one-to-one meeting with the founder of the organisation. The session was meant to last two hours. Mine went on for three as I had a lot to got off my chest and discuss.

That day and that woman transformed my life. At the end, she concluded that I should be an entrepreneur and professional (motivational) speaker. I thought that sounded very scary and I had no idea about how to become either, but I was up for giving it a go.

I will never forget the feeling as I walked a few miles from just off Pall Mall in central London, up the Mall, past Buckingham Palace and along to a party at a restaurant in the Chelsea area of the city. Even though I experienced every type of (British summer) weather – rain, hail, thunder, lightning, strong winds, sunshine and blue skies – I smiled all the way because I felt amazing and like I'd been given a new lease of life. I had rediscovered my new vocation and one which I have built up to give the rewarding and varied professional and personal life I have.

I started my first business with no financial backing and no idea of how to actually run a business. And, certainly during the first two years, I had an unnerving share of 'head in my hands' moments when I really thought that, financially, I was screwed. I had setbacks, some serious, but I also enjoyed some great successes. That's why, despite the former, I always knew I was doing something I not only loved but believed in. It's taken courage, action, determination, resilience, big hairy goals and persistence. And it's made me richer, in various ways.

REAL LIFE STORY

When Dorothy Stephenson started her own dance studio when she was 20 years old, no one took her seriously as she had always been the 'goofy' child who had grown up in a community where the arts weren't appreciated.

Dorothy recalled: 'My biggest hurdle was overcoming my insecurity as a young entrepreneur and proving, not only to those around me, but to myself, that I knew what I was doing. Overcoming that insecurity and gaining confidence has now led to a thriving and growing business that not only allows me to do what I love for a living, but also allows me to be a good role model for youth in the community.

'Many people who saw my business start and have seen it develop thought that I was too young to do such a thing when I did. Realistically, I didn't have a clue what I was doing, but I had it in me. I just took a leap of faith, pushed myself into it, and it was sink or swim. That, of course, doesn't fit all personalities, but it worked for me.

'Even if I didn't know exactly what I was doing, I would figure it out along the way. Not only that, confidence gave me the ability to stand up and be a role model and an image for my dancers and my community. You have to have confidence in yourself before others will have confidence in you, and in the profession that I'm in, and most professions for that matter, someone having confidence in you will definitely determine the success of your business.'

Dorothy concluded: 'When I was growing up, I had zero self-confidence. I was the dorky kid in school. Actually, that was my nickname – 'Dorky'. Kids picked on me constantly. There were days when I would go to the bathroom just to cry. Most days, actually. For 13 solid years, kids picked on me, pulled my hair, played cruel jokes on me, and it seemed that I was always alone. My life at home was no better. Both of my parents cared for me very much. The only problem was they were too busy fighting with each other to care about what I was doing.

'However, one lesson that my mother taught me was to always shoot for my dreams, and my father taught me to never back down. When I was in college, those two sayings just came out of nowhere and kicked me in the butt because I've been pushing toward my dreams ever since and I've never looked back. When I stepped into my five year high school reunion, my English teacher bellowed 'There's Dorothy! There's our class success story!' All those people who had picked on me all my life just stood there with their jaws dropped. It was great!'

REAL LIFE STORY

CJ lost her husband of seven and a half years to malignant melanoma. It shattered her hopes and her confidence.

'It is amazing the changes one's identity of self and personality go through when one loses a spouse. You get so used to sharing every decision and roadblock with that other person. When they are ripped away from you a part of you is now gone too and making decisions without them becomes almost impossible. Confidence in your own abilities are shaken to your very core,' said CJ.

'I am learning to do things on my own now. I installed a car stereo by myself for the very first time . . . and it worked! After losing a spouse, it is the little things like this that help boost my confidence. Every little thing I manage to do on my own now boosts my confidence a little bit more and with that boost of confidence I am finding it easier to handle the grief that I feel. It's taking the small steps that I can do successfully that is getting me closer to being able to take the big steps with confidence.'

Chapter 7

Sustaining confidence

Of all the cornerstones of confidence – action, belief, determination, resilience, acceptance, persistence, courage and a goal plan – action is the one that makes things happen. In other words, you have to actually do the things that you want or need to so you can achieve what you desire from life. Although all these facets of confidence complement each other, the simple fact is that you just have to Sod It! Face It! Do It!

You can read all the self-help and personal development books and articles possible, you can go on courses and you can pray that your confidence will increase so you can do something. But that alone will not make things happen for you. YOU have to take action and make things happen and, even though it may be unnerving or even frightening, YOU have to take that initial step. But it is YOU who will benefit at least tenfold when you have had a go at whatever you felt you didn't have the confidence for in the first place.

It's not as if you're doing something – whether asking for a pay rise from a grumpy boss or feeling sexually attractive when you're out of shape – that no one has experienced before. Millions and millions of other people have and will continue to go through the same doubts and dilemmas that you have been going through and will sometimes go through in the future.

Many have succeeded and grown in confidence in the process, as you have read in the real life stories and other examples included in this book. But that was only because they dreamed about what they really needed and wanted. They then summoned up the courage to take the action required to make something worthwhile happen in their lives and the lives of others. Even if they had setbacks, they were determined enough to persist in their aims. And this helped them become more resilient and self-accepting so they grew in their self-belief. This will have in turn strengthened their self-esteem and self-confidence, just as it will for you when you do the same.

Another important aspect is that you must not load the burden of expectation on yourself so, if you sometimes fall short, and you will, you do not castigate yourself. This will exert more pressure on you because you are more likely to feel you have failed in part or in whole.

Failure is proof that you are human, that you are brave and that you are living your life and not just existing.

Hope is a powerful and better alternative to expectation. It is the desire, but without the penalties. Just before a nerve-wracking and body-bashing martial arts grading test, a senior instructor told us to 'expect nothing but hope for everything'. How true that is because building and sustaining your confidence is about taking action by taking small steps and building upon those foundations, not just in the short-term, but for life. And I did hope … and got the higher belt grade too.

The good news is that the more you take action and just have a go at the things you want to tackle, but were once afraid of doing for fear of failing, then the more you will achieve because you've been strengthening your confidence core. It will become easier and your life will become more rewarding.

So, here are some further ways to help strengthen and sustain your confidence.

Action vitamins

Take one useful action every day, but at least once a week by doing something you want or need to do, no matter how simple, so you get into a routine of actively making a difference. Like the right vitamins, this will help strengthen your immunity to despondence and low self-esteem and self-confidence. Make this a habit so you train your brain to do it regularly enough so that it acts like it's on autopilot. The more you get used to doing something that once made you nervous or even nauseous, the less daunting and more doable it will become, making you more confident and capable.

Adventure

Your life is an adventure and adventure is about variety and stimulation. It's about trying new things, about absorbing as many useful and, ideally, harmless experiences as possible. Not viewing and acting as if life is an adventure and not living it that way is like driving through the world's most beautiful scenery while staring at the road or even the dashboard in front of you and ignoring the stunning environment of which you are now a part. You miss so much that would have made you feel and think differently.

Remember the wonderful quote that is a potent reminder of why we will regret not having a go at the challenges in our life. These may scare us and appear overwhelming, but the chances are we will achieve what we want if we have a go and enjoy being the person we want to be: 'Hell is the place where the person you are meets the person you could have been.'

It's a fact of your life and the lives of everyone else that you will experience good, bad and even bizarre times. Life should not be a series of experiences through which you just exist, trudging from one colourless day to another in which the only excitement and variety is when the office photocopier breaks down because someone sat on it to photocopy their splayed buttocks thereby cracking the glass surface and bending one of the delicate mechanisms. Not theirs – the machine's.

Now, interestingly, this Blunderbuss Buttocks was/is probably having more life adventure than you because they wanted to do something different and colourful that would break what can so easily become a seamless stream of subtle monotony. Now, please don't feel an urge to bare your briefs – or worse – and vault onto the office photocopier to print off some time-lapse style images of your briefs and/or bits. These machines malfunction when you least need them to – I mean, think of that report you've got to circulate to your colleagues and even clients. Instead of some, I'm sure, riveting facts, figures, fancy charts and graphs, you'll only be able to offer them an indelicate image of your delicate bits and, hard though it may seem, not everyone will be as excited or even as inflamed by this as you might vainly hope! This could lead to a caution for having overripe buttocks which, in turn, won't do your self-image and confidence any good.

Try to experience something new every month, if not every week. If you can do this every day, then wonderful. Whether it's getting to or from work by different means, changing something about your wardrobe, striking up a conversation with someone at your gym, signing up for a language course, starting a new hobby, planning something like a trip or an expedition to a new and unusual place – and we're not talking about a far-flung shopping centre with special offers on photocopier machines – you will add a new dimension to your life which will, in turn, reignite your senses and sense of purpose.

This enrichment, no matter how subtle, should make you realise that you have something worth living for, that life is full of opportunity and that you have the confidence and the right attitude to go out there and enjoy these things. As a result, you will feel better about yourself and that will help improve your confidence.

Mastermind group

Form a group of one to three really good, emotionally enlightened, positive and trustworthy friends who you can talk with about your challenges and successes. And they should be able to talk through their issues with you. This will give you another perspective, as well as providing a cathartic release for any issues you have that affect your confidence. In addition, you will gain confidence from the fact that your friends trust you and your judgement on how you can help tackle your issues.

Agree to meet up in places that make you all feel good and at ease, where you can talk openly and be heard. This could be a boutique coffee shop or a local deer park, for instance.

Laughter

Laughter is one of life's greatest joys. It can make us feel amused, happy, loved, warm, positive, physically healthier, sexy, admired and desired. It is one of the most important aspects of any successful life and relationship. So try to laugh at least once a day either with someone funny and/or at something like a film, a comedy show or a scenario that you find amusing.

Research has shown that:

- Laughter may reduce your risk of cardiovascular disease. Researchers have found that laughter is linked to the healthy functioning of blood vessels by causing the inner lining to expand, increasing blood flow.[12]

- Laughing just 15 minutes a day can help you lose weight. Scientists have discovered that a daily dose of chuckling can burn up to five pounds of fat over a year. Ten to 15 minutes of laughter could increase energy expenditure by 10 to 40 calories per day.[13]

- A good laugh stimulates your organs, soothes tension and tummy aches, improves your immune system, relieves pain and increases personal satisfaction.[14]

- The levels of two stress hormones, cortisol and epinephrine, which suppress the body's immune system, will actually drop after a dose of laughter.

- There's now scientific proof that laughter is contagious. Researchers have found that hearing laughter and other positive sounds triggers a response in the area of the brain that is activated when we smile.[15]

- Laughter causes positive changes in brain chemistry by releasing endorphins, and it brings more oxygen into the body with the deeper inhalations.

- Laughter releases anger, fear, guilt, anxiety and tension.

- Laughter encourages concentration on 'right' attitudes rather than 'wrong' attitudes.

- Higher levels of an antibody (salivary immunoglobulin A) that fights infectious organisms entering the respiratory tract were found in the saliva of people who watched humorous videos or experienced good moods.

- Researchers found that after watching an hour-long video of slapstick comedy the 'natural killer cells', which seek out and destroy malignant cells, more actively attacked tumour cells in test tubes. And these effects lasted up to 12 hours.[16]

- Studies show that a great sense of humour can add an additional eight years to your life.[17]

- Pre-school children laugh or smile 400 times a day. However, that number drops to only 15 by the time people reach age 35.[18]

- People smile only 35% as much as they think they do.[19]

■ A survey by Hodge-Cronin & Associates found that of 737 CEOs surveyed, 98% preferred job candidates with a sense of humour to those without. Another survey indicated that 84% of the executives thought that employees with a sense of humour do a better job than people with little or no sense of humour.

In short, laughter is great for your mental and physical well-being and so spending time with people and putting yourself in situations where you are made to laugh, as well as making other people chuckle, will make you feel better about life and help with your levels of confidence.

Location, location, location

Change your environment when you can to somewhere soothing and/or inspiring. For instance, if you work from home or are looking after kids all day, go to a popular and busy part of town to soak up a more active and fast paced tempo of life. You will think differently. Alternatively, escape to some beautiful countryside, the sea or a peaceful lake or river.

Research shows that the sound of waves alters the wave patterns in our brains, as does the sound of water which can allow us to slide into a deeply calm and relaxed state. And similar research has shown that being in the countryside is better for your mental health.[20] It is calming and, because of the naturalness of the environment, it is more inspiring and comforting than the higher octane town and city, which can sometimes be too abrasive.

Inspiring inventory

Draw up a list of with two columns. In one, write down the varying qualities you have, no matter how small. This could be that you're funny, that you have a good general knowledge, that you're great with children, that you're good at crossword puzzles or even that you've got a fantastic bottom … or other brilliant bits!

In the other column write down the successes you have had. These could include getting a great new job, saving someone's life, getting fantastic grades at school, bungee jumping from a perilous height when others were too scared to do it or that you have been promoted or rewarded at work. Don't limit it. Let your memory and your pen or keyboard run riot.

Then, carry this list around with you, or at least have copies close to hand, to remind you when you feel low and unsure that you have many reasons to be confident. You will see just how much you have to offer. And the more you refer to this the more your subconscious mind will strengthen your own perception of just how confident you have reason to be and this will guide how you come across to others.

Your Life Rule

Reappraise your Life Rule. These are rules created by your beliefs, which are based on your experiences from early life until the present day. So if you have lost your job you will probably be telling yourself that you are unworthy of employment and not very successful or appealing to other employers. That rule-cum-mantra will subconsciously direct how you think, feel and act, and therefore how others will think and feel about you and how they act with you.

Anxiety is caused whenever such life experiences are triggered by something negative or hurtful that somebody says or by a bad event. Your rules provide what appears to be a coping strategy. In this situation you take precautions, like adhering to a superstition. But these only maintain low self-esteem because you don't know if the situation would have been avoided without taking such precautions. Research has shown that 50% of how we react to things is genetic which means that the remainder is largely down to our experiences and, most importantly, how we decide to deal with them.

So try changing that to something positive and less harsh. It could be something like:

> *'I am a person of many gifts and have a lot to offer the world. I have strengths and weaknesses like everyone else and I might have setbacks, but I have had and will have more successes. That's why people love and like me for who I am, just the way I am.'*

Read this out loud at least a couple of times a day for a week, or more if you need to, so it conditions your mind to believe it and act upon it. It's about creating your own Life Rule and helping to reappraise your beliefs about yourself.

Movies and music

- Watch movies and play music that not only make you feel good, but that also make you feel as if you will achieve what you want and need to against the odds.

- Play movies and music that make you realise the good things in your life, from your attributes to your friends.

- Play movies and material that makes you laugh.

Mind movies

Making your own movie with you as the glowing star who does whatever you script yourself to do is a very powerful way of gearing your mind and body to be what you envisage yourself being. Visualising something clearly often helps it seem more possible and increases our motivation to achieve it.

Visualising ourselves successfully performing some task and reaching a successful outcome can help us overcome mental barriers to success. It's important to make these movies as vivid as possible with lots of colour, sounds, feelings and, where applicable, dialogue. You write the script, direct the camera and the actors and create the vibe.

There are two ways to do it:

- One is using the first person view. You see yourself through your own eyes in the movie and experience everything as you would in reality.

- The second is the third person view. You see yourself through the eyes of another person there in the movie.

Both techniques are powerful because your mind and body experiences what it is like to achieve what you want to. But some research suggests that using the third person makes you 20% more successful than the first person approach.

In a controlled experiment, students in Australia who had never shot a basketball used mental imagery to learn how to shoot baskets.[21] During later tests, those only using imagery shot as accurately as students who practised shooting real basketballs. This technique is used by many top athletes and others who perform in public.

Before an important event many of the world's top performers imagine themselves in a desired situation, visualising how it will look, sound and feel. Our minds and bodies are intimately linked in what is known as a cybernetic loop (our nervous system's communication mechanism). This is where our nerve impulses travel both from the mind to the body and back the other way. So your body will be affected by how you're thinking and vice-versa.

You can use your cybernetic loop to your advantage by altering your body posture, eye movement, physical movements and breathing to influence, change or maintain your desired mental state. For example, if you took quick shallow breaths for a few minutes you would start to feel anxious. But if you took slower, deeper breaths, you would feel less on edge.

Therefore whatever you think affects the way your body feels and this in turn gives off a vibe, which those you perform in front of and deal with will sense. So in turn they will unconsciously respond to how you feel about yourself and that can affect the outcome of what you're doing.

But it's vital that you have a balanced movie plot where you experience not just the good things you want, but also the setbacks and how you overcome them. Some research has shown that just visualising a utopian world where everything is amazing, like better exam results, promotions at work or potentially perfect partners practically falling out of trees, kitchen cupboards and elsewhere unexpected, will not always help you because you rely on fantasy more than reality.

Experiments have been done where people had to fantasise about their perfect scenario and then later think about the possible hurdles and challenges. These people were more successful than those who focused just on the fantasy.[22]

Three great things

At the end of every day, remind yourself of at least three things that happened to you that were nice or great, no matter how subtle or unusual. Even when you've had a bad day, there will have been positive experiences. It could have been the good-looking person in the street who just smiled at you out of the blue as you passed them. It could be the fact that you made someone laugh or were made to laugh. It could be that you saw a stunning sunset. It could be that your train arrived on time so you didn't have to wait. It could be that you read a story in the newspaper that inspired you. We have experiences every day that can remind us of what abundance we have in our lives. In reality, you will probably find many more.

Is that all!

There's a very good chance that irritations, setbacks and disasters will happen. In fact, it's a lifetime guarantee that they will! That is the unpredictability of the reality of life. When you feel you can't go on, does your life stop dead in its tracks? Do you stop breathing or does your body stop working? Are you swept off life's stage with a large brush before you can say goodbye to people? Will you not learn from and be changed in any way as a result of this experience? No. Not at all. The planet will continue to turn on its axis and you will still be here. So, you can stand around and mope and moan. But not only does that not achieve anything that will help you redress the situation, it also won't look or sound good.

That setback or disaster will not define your whole life because not only will you have had other setbacks and disasters, you have also had many successes. Setbacks are a facet of everyday life for millions of people around the world. It is a question of accepting your fallibility and faults as well as rejoicing in and reminding yourself of your strengths and successes.

Toxic people audit

The only difference between toxic people and toxic waste is that the latter has warning signs plastered all over it. The even more alarming thing is that some toxic people can do a very good superficial job of appearing to be your friend. After spending time with them you can sometimes feel rather drained, negative or joyless. This feeling can creep up on you without you realising and it means you don't necessarily pin the cause on them. That's understandable as you realise that they can often be nice, but there is a negative vibe about people like this who are invariably self-absorbed and see their life in too negative a fashion.

Your encouraging words and acts of support will disappear down the plughole that is their self-absorbed attitude filter. So you give more … and more … and more, but you can't compete with this black hole of negativity. This will adversely affect your self-worth and self-confidence. And it will be exacerbated by the fact that they can and will latch onto you as they see you as a plentiful source of sympathy and support, even though they may never take advantage of your advice and encouragement. But they will, in the process, take advantage of you. So handle toxic people with care and do not bring them into or keep them in your life.

Helping others

Too many people are out for just themselves in this Me Me society in which we now live. So, if you're actually someone who gives to people without an invoice or an unsubtle hint about some form of payback, then you benefit in a way that takers won't.

Giving someone some useful advice, contacts, an understanding ear or financial support, without any expectation of reciprocation, can provide you with a power derived from a warm sense of altruism. Most of the time, the recipient will be very grateful and will probably want to find a way to reciprocate your giving.

It will make you stand out from so many people who, in wanting to better their lot in life, get so bogged down in the It's All About Me approach rather than thinking about those around them. Instead of asking how you are and meaning it, they're preoccupied with how they're going to make their next bit of money, how they're going to conjure up their next party night invite so they don't have an awkwardly blank look on their face when someone asks them what they're doing on Saturday night, or how they're going to look engaging and engaged at some social or other occasion instead of looking wrapped up in themselves.

So it's understandable why anyone who gives and puts other people first is going to be popular and well thought of which, in turn, will make them feel and act in a more confident way. In my professional and personal experience, 99% of people are too worried about what they say, how they look, what other people think about them and how they come across. The clever 1% are genuinely interested in what the other person thinks and feels. They are the ones who get what they want because of how they make others feel. And that makes the givers more confident which, in turn, rubs off on those that they give to.

Research has found that those who spent a higher percentage of their income on others were far happier than those who spent it on themselves.[23] And in other research people performed five acts of non-financial kindness each week for six weeks (e.g. writing a thank you note, giving blood, helping a friend, etc.). Some performed one act each day and experienced a small increase in happiness. Others performed all the acts on one day and enjoyed a 40% increase in happiness![24]

Celebration

Celebrate your successes, no matter how small. Reward yourself for achieving a target or some other form of success. And the more significant your successes are, then the more significant your treat can be. Such rewards create positive emotions around taking action and achieving and act as a warm, encouraging and empowering incentive to try to achieve more, thereby helping sustain your confidence.

Getting Seán Brickell to work with you

You will find invaluable information as well as details about Seán Brickell's keynote speaking, masterclasses, coaching and facilitating, his business consultancy services as well as his growing range of products on personal and professional confidence and communication at www.SeanBrickell.com.

References

1. Ong, A. D., Bergeman, C. S., Bisconti, T. L. and Wallace, K. A. (2006) 'Psychological resilience, positive emotions, and successful adaptation to stress in later life'. *Journal of Personality and Social Psychology*, 91(4): 730–49. Tugade, M. M., Fredrickson, B. L. and Barrett, L. F. (2004) 'Psychological resilience and positive emotional granularity: Examining the benefits of positive emotions on coping and health'. *Journal of Personality*, 72(6): 1161–90.

2. Tugade, M. M., Fredrickson, B. L. and Barrett, L. F. (2004) 'Psychological resilience and positive emotional granularity: Examining the benefits of positive emotions on coping and health'. *Journal of Personality*, 72(6): 1161–90.

3. Ong, A. D., Bergeman, C. S., Bisconti, T. L. and Wallace, K. A. (2006) 'Psychological resilience, positive emotions, and successful adaptation to stress in later life'. *Journal of Personality and Social Psychology*, 91(4): 730–49. Tugade, M. M., Fredrickson, B. L. and Barrett, L. F. (2004) 'Psychological resilience and positive emotional granularity: Examining the benefits of positive emotions on coping and health'. *Journal of Personality*, 72(6): 1161–90.

4. Lyubomirsky, S., Schkade, D. and Sheldon, K. M. (2005) 'Pursuing Happiness: The Architecture of Sustainable Change'. *Review of General Psychology*, 9(2): 111–31.

5. Gilovich, T. and Husted Medvec, V. (1995) 'The experience of regret: What, when, and why'. *Psychological Review*, 102: 379–95. Gilovich, T. and Husted Medvec, V. (1994) 'The Temporal Pattern to the Experience of Regret'. *Journal of Personality and Social Psychology*, 67(3): 357–65.

6. Parks, M. (2006) *Workplace Romance: Poll Findings.* Alexandria, VA: Society for Human Resource Management and CareerJournal.com. www.lrgllc.com/rpubs/7.pdf

7. 'Standing up to the bullies' (2007). *Safety Management* (June): 45–6. www.businesswings.co.uk/articles/Bullying-in-the-workplace—too-costly-to-ignore

8. Kruger, J. and Dunning, D. (1999) 'Unskilled and Unaware of It: How Difficulties in Recognizing One's Own Incompetence Lead to Inflated Self-Assessments'. *Journal of Personality and Social Psychology*, 77(6): 1121–34.

9. Jones, E. E. and Gordon, E. M. (1972) 'Timing of self-disclosure and its effects on personal attraction'. *Journal of Personality and Social Psychology*, 24(3) December: 358–65.

10. Valenzuela, A. and Raghubir, P. (2007) 'The Role of Strategy in Mixed-Gender Group Interactions: A Study of the Television Show *The Weakest Link*. *Sex Roles: A Journal of Research*, 57(3&4) August: 293–303.

11. McCullough, M. E., Root, L. M. and Cohen, A. D. (2006) 'Writing About the Benefits of an Interpersonal Transgression Facilitates Forgiveness'. *Journal of Consulting and Clinical Psychology*, 74(5): 887–97.

12. University of Maryland Medical Center, Baltimore (2000) 'Laughter Is Good for Your Heart'. News Release. www.umm.edu/news/releases/laughter.htm

13. Colmenares, C. (2005) 'No joke: Study finds laughing can burn calories'. *Reporter: Vanderbilt University Medical Center's Weekly Newspaper*, 10 June. www.mc.vanderbilt.edu/reporter/index.html?ID=4030

14. Mayo Clinic 'Stress relief from laughter? Yes, no joke'.
www.mayoclinic.com/health/stress-relief/SR00034

15. Wellcome Trust (2006) 'Research: Laughter is contagious'. 13
December.
www.wellcome.ac.uk/News/2006/News/WTX034943.htm

16. 'Laughter Yoga'.
www.livingwithrheumatoidarthritis.com/LaughterYoga.html

17. 'Laughter facts'. www.humor-laughter.com/laughter-facts.html

18. 'Laughter Yoga'.
www.livingwithrheumatoidarthritis.com/LaughterYoga.html

19. 'Laughter facts'. www.humor-laughter.com/laughter-facts.html

20. Weich, S., Twigg, L., Lewis, G. and Jones, K. (2005) 'Geographical
variation in rates of common mental disorders in Britain: prospective
cohort study'. *The British Journal of Psychiatry,* 187: 29–34.

21. Chilton, P. (2001) 'Mental Imagery'.
www.odysseyofthesoul.org/freomm/mentaimagery.htm

22. Oettingen, G. and Mayer, D. (2002) 'The motivating function of
thinking about the future: Expectations versus fantasies'. *Journal of
Personality and Social Psychology*, 83: 1198–212.

23. Dunn, E. W., Aknin, L. B. and Norton, M. I. (2008) 'Spending money
on others promotes happiness'. *Science*, 319: 1687–88.

24. Lyubomirsky, S., Schkade, D. and Sheldon, K. M. (2005) 'Pursuing
Happiness: The Architecture of Sustainable Change'. *Review of
General Psychology*, 9(2): 111–31.

Index

Some other titles from How To Books

CHALLENGING DEPRESSION AND DESPAIR
A self-help, medication-free programme that will change your life

ANGELA PATMORE

This book is offered as a lifeline to people at the bottom of the bottomless pit of depression.

It will explain the research and the thinking behind the 'tough love' approach, much of which may be new to you because it flies in the face of current trends. With positive, common sense strategies, this book enables you to regain emotional control, showing that it is possible to combat depression without resorting to drugs or costly and often ineffective therapy.

The first part of the book offers fresh insights into depression and into how it can be overcome. The second offers practical advice culminating in a series of challenges that will enable you to change your entire attitude to emotional health and achieve a more positive and hopeful outlook on life.

To be of any real use to someone in despair, a self-help programme must provide, step by step, a practical stairway out of hell. This is that stairway.

ISBN 978-1-84528-439-8

FREE YOURSELF FROM ANXIETY
A self-help guide to overcoming anxiety disorders

EMMA FLETCHER AND MARTHA LANGLEY

'I firmly believe that this book could help sufferers take control of their anxiety. The book is written in a very sensible and practical way. There are lots of handy hints and tips given to each chapter. I ended up reading it from cover to cover.'
www.talkeczema.com

'Easy to understand...well laid out...this book tells you how. There is so much help, support and information in this book...I was very impressed.'
No Panic Newsletter

ISBN 978-1-84528-311-7

HOW TO MANAGE DIFFICULT PEOPLE
Proven strategies for dealing with challenging management relationships at work

ALAN FAIRWEATHER

Dealing with difficult customers, colleagues, uncooperative staff, a manipulative boss - or an irritating neighbour - is a challenge many people face on a day-to-day basis. People in business are now under extreme pressure to make things happen, get more sales and turn a profit. This constant pressure or fear can make people difficult to deal with. This book shows you how to identify and understand awkward and challenging behaviours and how to manage them.

ISBN 978-1-84528-391-9

Ordering

How To Books are available through all good bookshops, or you can order direct from us through Grantham Book Services.

Tel: +44 (0)1476 541080
Fax: +44 (0)1476 541061
Email: orders@gbs.tbs-ltd.co.uk

Or via our website
www.howtobooks.co.uk

To order via any of these methods please quote the title(s) of the book(s) and your credit card number together with its expiry date.

For further information about our books and catalogue, please contact:
How To Books
Spring Hill House
Spring Hill Road
Begbroke
Oxford
OX5 1RX

Visit our web site at
www.howtobooks.co.uk

Or you can contact us by email at **info@howtobooks.co.uk**